Indiana's African-American Heritage

Indiana's African-American Heritage:

Essays from *Black History News & Notes*

Edited by Wilma L. Gibbs

Second Edition

Indiana Historical Society Press
Indianapolis 2007

First edition published in 1993. Second edition 2007

Printed in the United States of America

This book is a publication of the
Indiana Historical Society Press
450 West Ohio Street
Indianapolis, Indiana 46202-3269 USA
www.indianahistory.org
Telephone orders 1-800-447-1830
Fax orders 317-234-0562
Online orders @ shop.indianahistory.org

The paper in this publication meets the minimum requirements of American National Standard for Information Sciences—Permanence of Paper for Printed Library Materials. ANSI Z 39.48–1984

Library of Congress Cataloging-in-Publication Data

Indiana's African-American heritage: essays from Black history news & notes / edited by Wilma L. Gibbs
p. cm.
Includes bibliographical references and index.
ISBN 0-87195-098-7 (cloth): $27.95—ISBN 0-87195-099-5 (paper): $16.95
1. Afro-Americans—Indiana—History. I. Gibbs, Wilma L. II. Black history news & notes.
F535.N4153 1993
977.2'000496073—dc20 93-19282
CIP

To my parents, William J. and Tessie A. Gibbs, who taught me early that truth and knowledge, and by inference, history, would set you free.

Contents

Foreword

The Negro, Carter G. Woodson always insisted, had a heroic past of which all blacks should be proud. Retrieving and studying that history was an indispensable prerequisite to the advancement of blacks in the United States. Woodson worked tirelessly toward this end as founder of the Association for the Study of Negro Life and History, founder and editor of the *Journal of Negro History*, and originator of Negro History Week. Woodson called on an audience at Hampton Institute in 1921 to study its history "with the understanding that we are not, after all, an inferior people. . . . We are going back to that beautiful history and it is going to inspire us to greater achievements. It is not going to be long before we can so sing the story to the outside world as to convince it of the value of our history . . . and we are going to be recognized as men."[1] One does not have to subscribe totally to Woodson's motivation or objectives to agree with his clarion call for the study of black history. There is something intrinsically valuable about the study of a people's history, especially a people who have been the victims of widespread oppression. There is no doubt that we have come a long way in the years since Woodson issued his call. Woodson, I suspect, would be pleasantly surprised by the advances made in both the reach and sophistication of African-American history.

Some of the credit for these advances has to be given to state and local historians, professionals and amateurs, who have spent countless hours piecing together the history of black communities and institutions. In the case of Indiana this task was made more difficult by the scarcity of sources. In the late 1970s the Indiana Historical Society committed itself to the retrieval, collection, and preservation of documents related to the history of African-Americans in the state. The success of such an initiative required the timely publication of research findings. In order to meet this need the Society decided to publish *Black History News & Notes,* an occasional newsletter that first appeared in October 1979. It aimed through short articles, information on new acquisitions, queries from readers, book reviews, and announcements of events to generate interest in and research on Indiana black history. It has done just that. While its format has been reorganized, and its publication schedule regularized, *Black History News & Notes* has remained true to its original objectives. Most importantly, it has encouraged research in black Indiana history. This small volume consists of articles that first appeared in its pages. It is, in many ways, a testimonial to those who saw the need for such a publication. Among the authors are professional and amateur historians, graduate students, and professionals from other walks of life, all with one interest: furthering research in the state's black history.

These articles cover a wide range of topics including the church, rural and urban communities, education, cultural institutions, newspapers, women's history, and biography. In one form or another all address the question of how an oppressed people confront a system that denies them their basic human rights and how, in resisting, they make space for themselves, space in which the expressions of their talents are possible. Self and community improvement and autonomy are the themes that bind these essays together. The actors call to us across the reach of history to understand their commitment to equality and to the twin strategies of "protest and build" they employed to attain their objectives. When Madam C. J. Walker was denied entry to an Indianapolis movie theater, she protested against the exclusion and committed resources to the building of a theater to which all would be admitted. It would be wrong, I think, to see Walker's actions simply as an acceptance of the racial status quo; she was simultaneously demanding her rights as a citizen to be admitted to a public place, and at the same time recognizing the fact that someone had to cater to the needs of African-Americans in the city. As Gloria J. Gibson-Hudson shows, Walker's actions, with the resolve of her daughter A'Lelia and business manager F. B. Ransom, led to the establishment of an important cultural center in the capital, one which offered films, vaudeville, jazz, and local talent shows. Conceived out of a protest against segregation, the establishment of the center showed that blacks had the talent and means to build their own institutions.

Like other Americans, blacks have placed enormous store in education as a vehicle of social progress. It is, as many in the nineteenth century were fond of saying, the wheel that turned the car of progress. H. J. Lewis, born a slave in Mississippi in 1837, was self-taught, Marvin Jeter tells us. By the time Lewis joined the staff of the *Indianapolis Freeman* in 1889 he had already established a reputation as a first-rate illustrator, cartoonist, and engraver. Samuel M. Plato was equally determined. Born in Alabama, Plato moved to Marion in 1902. There he lived for almost two decades during which time he established a reputation as an architect and builder of churches, homes, and public buildings. Many of the public buildings he designed in other parts of the country are on the National Register of Historic Places. William E. Scott, painter and muralist, was born in Indianapolis in 1884 and attended local schools. With the encouragement of his mentor, Scott enrolled at the Chicago Art Institute during which time he painted murals at five public school buildings in the city. Scott went to France in 1909 where he studied with one of America's masters, Henry O. Tanner, who had escaped the debilitating racism of the United States for the relative freedom of France. Scott's works were also exhibited in Paris and London. Later in life the Indianapolis Public School Board commissioned Scott to paint murals in city schools.

All of these individual accomplishments were built on a tradition of community effort to improve educational opportunities. During the antebellum period, when blacks were increasingly denied their rights, the AME church, Lori Jacobi shows, provided the rudiments of an educational system. Church leaders agonized over the need for a seminary to provide congregations with a better educated ministry. The periodical *Repository of Religion and Literature and of Science,* published between 1858 and 1861, was seen as an important vehicle for the expression of the community's literary talents. The struggle for equal access to public schools at no time precluded the need to cater to the educational needs of black children. It was a battle that had to be fought on two fronts. African-Americans had to pressure white America to live up to its declared principles of equality for all, and, at the same time, provide those services denied their communities. They educated themselves while demanding equal access to state schools. A measure of victory would be achieved in 1869 when a state law opened schools to all. Given this history, it should come as no surprise that so many blacks resisted efforts to segregate Indianapolis, Gary, and Evansville high schools in the early 1920s. As had been done elsewhere, the Indianapolis Public School Board tried to mollify opponents of segregation with the promise that black schools would lead to the employment of black teachers. As Stanley Warren shows, Indianapolis blacks agonized over the utility of promoting a black high school in a segregated society. To relent in the face of segregationist pressures, on the one hand, was to concede one of the basic tenets of the struggle for equality. But to ignore political reality in the face of a rising tide of segregationist legislation, on the other hand, ran the risk of losing all opportunity to influence policy. It was a dilemma in no way unique to Indianapolis. Blacks in many other parts of the country had been struggling with similar issues since the first wave of desegregation agitation at the end of the Civil War. The community reluctantly accepted reality and marshaled its energies to make Crispus Attucks the best high school in the state. The acceptance of that reality, however, in no way diminished the community's desire to be rid of segregation.

In the face of segregationist pressures the black community in Indianapolis united around the need to erect institutions that catered to its particular needs. The tradition was established even before a community became clearly identifiable in the capital. Like so many other historians of small antebellum urban black communities (blacks were less than 5 percent of the city's population), Earline Rae Ferguson has difficulty identifying the exact contours of the city's black community. There is even some doubt that there was a spatially identifiable black community in this period. Yet as Jacobi shows, blacks nonetheless felt a need to build their own churches. In the mid-1840s the Reverend William Paul Quinn reported a dramatic growth of the AME church in Indiana and Illinois: forty-seven churches with two thousand worshippers, fifty Sunday schools, regular camp meetings, and forty temperance societies. Away from the capital city in Greencastle, Putnam County, Arnold Cooper provides a glimpse into the organization of a small AME congregation at a time when the black population stood at roughly 105. Begun as a "Methodist Mission" in 1872, the church catered to the needs of a handful of members who met first in a home then in a room above a store before raising the money to buy St. Benedict's Catholic Church in 1878.

Institutional building was not limited to urban and small-town Indiana. As Xenia Cord shows, there were more than twenty black rural settlements in the years before the Civil War. Most of the settlers (many of whom were of mixed race) were born in North Carolina and moved to Indiana to avoid that southern state's increasingly restrictive laws. They settled first in southern Indiana counties, later fanning out into frontier areas. Often with the aid of nearby Quakers, many of whom had left North Carolina for a similar reason, these black rural settlers established their own churches and schools.

Institutional building is in many ways a community's declaration of its autonomy. It also provides the means by which a community can marshal its energies to attack specific problems. Cooper, for example, shows the extent to which a community-based organization (in this case the small Greencastle AME church) could be galvanized on relatively short notice to come to the aid of those in need. Between November 1879 and January 1880 the church and its pastor played an active role in attracting and welcoming 250 blacks from North Carolina to the town. Similarly Julius Holder used the *Evansville Argus* to promote self-determination, particularly the development and control of black businesses in the city. He consistently called on blacks to patronize these businesses and those owned by whites who employed blacks. The *Argus* supported the National Association for the Advancement of Colored People's (NAACP) boycott of local merchants who refused to hire blacks and its campaign for school desegregation.

The history of institutional building cries out for a deeper understanding of the men and women who were the driving force behind these community efforts. A number of the biographical articles provide some clues to people like the Reverends Quinn and John H. Clay of the small church in Greencastle. But we know little about the many others, especially the women who, as Emma Lou Thornbrough and Ferguson show, played such vital roles in community efforts. Thornbrough points us to the difficulty. The successes of present-day community efforts, she writes, "rest on the patient, unselfish, oftentimes unrewarding and largely forgotten efforts of earlier generations of anonymous black women whom history has overlooked." How to identify and locate information on these women are major challenges in our efforts to unravel the past. Woman's activities, Thornbrough shows, ranged from moral uplift, social improvement, including better health care, and expanding educational opportunities to the struggle against segregation. Women worked to build schools, hospitals, and charity organizations and were involved simultaneously in the fight for political and civil rights. Ferguson answers Thornbrough's call for more research on black women in her article on Lillian Thomas Fox. Born in Chicago in 1866, Fox settled in Indianapolis in the early 1880s. An elocutionist and journalist for both black and white city newspapers, Fox was the founder of the Woman's Improvement Club, which played a prominent role in the fight against tuberculosis, and was a major force in the formation of the Indiana State Federation of Colored Women's Clubs. Her weekly column in the *Indianapolis News* (which, incidentally, did not permit her to write under her own byline) remains an invaluable source of black community activities in the period.

Much more needs to be done. In her wide-ranging and informative article Thornbrough suggests interesting avenues of future research in black women's history. Any graduate student who reads this article comes away with a number of possible dissertation topics. For example, there is still a need for a history of black women's clubs, local chapters of the NAACP, and the role of women in the struggle against segregation. As Wilma Gibbs shows, the Black Women in the Middle West Project aimed to generate interest in local black history in an effort to collect the documents needed to address Thornbrough's suggested lines of inquiry. The project is a blueprint for community involvement in the collection and preservation of black history. Generally these records have not been preserved, and where they have, owners have been understandably reluctant to part with invaluable family records. The project, which was built on the active involvement of black citizens throughout the state, has unearthed invaluable materials which have been preserved and made available to scholars.

Darrel Bigham suggests other areas for possible research. His article on the *Evansville Argus* gives us a glimpse into the central role of a newspaper in a community's life. It is, at one and the same time, observer, booster, and gadfly, a combination of roles not easily achieved. Yet Bigham laments the fact that little is known of the paper's forceful editor, Julius Holder. We need to know much more about the many newspapers published in the state. Cord, in her article on black applicants to the Cherokee Restitution Appropriation, takes up the call for more research in a very inventive way. Using records generated by the 1906 Cherokee Restitution Act, under which anyone of Cherokee descent whose ancestors were deprived of property during resettlement could apply for reparations, she shows what a rich source this is for genealogical research. Many of the early black settlers from North Carolina claimed Cherokee ancestry, and although their claims were overwhelmingly rejected the records do help us to piece together some early migration patterns.

Given its record one wonders why other historical societies with statewide missions have not followed the lead of *Black History News & Notes*. While research into the history of African-Americans in some other states has been more extensive, the existence of a publication like *Black History News & Notes* has been a boon to those in Indiana interested in local history. The articles it publishes continue slowly but perceptively to broaden our knowledge of Indiana African-American history. While the picture that emerges from the blending together of these scattered dots is broader than anything Carter G. Woodson could have imagined, it depicts a past of resolve and struggle in the face of frightful odds; an heroic past.

R. J. M. Blackett
Indiana University
Bloomington, Indiana

Note

1. Quoted in August Meier and Elliott Rudwick, *Black History and the Historical Profession, 1915–1980* (Urbana: University of Illinois Press, 1986), 9.

Acknowledgments

The completion of this project has been a team effort. It has relied heavily upon the scholarship, support, and cooperation of the thirteen authors who contributed their essays. In his foreword, Richard Blackett does an admirable job of binding together sixteen essays that examine the antebellum period to the present and the state from the north to the south. All of the essays are subsumed under five broad subheadings related to Indiana African-American history: education and culture, women's history, cities and rural communities, biographies, and historical source materials.

I am indebted to Peter T. Harstad, executive director of the Indiana Historical Society, who a few years ago suggested that selected articles from the quarterly newsletter, *Black History News & Notes* (*BHN&N*) be published individually. The idea of an anthology germinated from that initial suggestion. The essays in this volume originally appeared in *BHN&N.*

I appreciate the efforts of library staff members who did some of the preliminary preparation work of the manuscript, including Susan Darnell, Barbara McCurdy, and my summer student assistant Courtney DeMoss. Several former Visual Collections staff, Carolyn Autry, Joan Hostetler, Lisa Lussier, and Deborah Markisohn, were helpful as I selected photographic support for the newsletter and subsequently for this volume. Under the general supervision of Curator Stephen Fletcher, Susan Sutton, visual collections coordinator, gave me her expert help, aided by the technical assistance of photographer Kim Ferrill. Leigh Darbee, curator of printed collections, should be commended for her active efforts and cooperation in collection-building in the area of Indiana African-American history over the past decade. I have also felt the uncompromised support and encouragement of my supervisor, Alexandra S. Gressitt, curator of manuscripts and archives, and Bruce L. Johnson, library director. Manuscripts Department colleagues Paul Brockman and Charles Latham, along with the rest of the library staff, lent their moral support.

More than any other individual, my gratitude for support of this book goes to Paula Corpuz, senior editor at the Society, who regularly assists with the quarterly publication of *BHN&N*. An "editor's editor," Corpuz plowed through the manuscript with vigor and efficiency. She was ably assisted by Publications Division staff members Kathy Breen, Shirley McCord, and Megan McKee. Thanks also to Thomas A. Mason, director of publications, who helped with the "big picture view" of the project.

I would be remiss if I failed to thank other Society staff: Raymond L. Shoemaker, who made me think from my initial employment interview with him that the Society would be a great place to work; Connie McBirney, who helped me get the bugs out of my computer and who exemplifies the cooperative spirit that exists at the institution; Carolyn Smith, membership secretary, who manages the distribution of the newsletter; Thomas K. Krasean, who coordinates the Society's annual meetings (these have provided additional forums for many articles appearing in *BHN&N*); and Robert M. Taylor, Jr., who has encouraged me in various writing projects. I am very grateful to the Society's trustees, who provide an atmosphere where staff can creatively "collect, preserve, interpret, and disseminate documentary and visual evidence and support scholarly research" as they promote public awareness and the appreciation of Indiana history. Special thanks goes to Stanley Warren, who has the distinction of being a member of the Society's board of trustees and a contributor to this volume.

Several individuals, many on behalf of their institutions, supplied photographic support for the book. I am grateful to them as well as to the people who are in the loop of the Black History Program—donors of materials; members of the Society who select black history as an interest group; and researchers of Indiana African-American history. Many thanks to the library pioneers who conceived and acted upon the idea of a Black History Collecting Project and newsletter. The list includes Tom Rumer, Jeff Gunderson, and Steve Vincent. My predecessor, Donald West, built upon their work. The Collecting Project began under the capable Society administration of Gayle Thornbrough. All of these parts have contributed to the success of the program. Hoosiers at home and beyond the borders of Indiana should be proud of *BHN&N,* a unique publication.

Finally, thanks go to my daughters Johari and Jamila Miller, mature and seasoned students and good human beings. They make me smile and remind me on those days that ask or answer questions that God's grace is boundless.

Wilma L. Gibbs

Contributors

Darrel E. Bigham, professor of history and director of the Historic Southern Indiana Project, University of Southern Indiana, Evansville, Indiana

Arnold Cooper, professor and chair of the Department of Education, Lincoln University, Jefferson City, Missouri

Xenia E. Cord, researcher, historian, and folklorist, Kokomo, Indiana

Earline Rae Ferguson, Ph.D. student in history, Indiana University, Bloomington, Indiana

Arville L. Funk, late attorney of Corydon, Indiana

Wilma L. Gibbs, program archivist and editor of *Black History News & Notes,* Indiana Historical Society, Indianapolis, Indiana

Gloria J. Gibson-Hudson, assistant professor of Afro-American Studies and assistant director of the Black Film Center/Archive, Indiana University, Bloomington, Indiana

Lori B. Jacobi, Ph.D. student in history, Indiana University, Bloomington, Indiana

Marvin D. Jeter, archaeologist, Arkansas Archeological Survey, Monticello, Arkansas

Katherine M. Jourdan, regional director, West Virginia State Historic Preservation Office, Wheeling, West Virginia

William E. Taylor, lecturer in black art history, Afro-American Studies, Indiana University-Purdue University, Indianapolis, Indiana, and Indiana University, Bloomington, Indiana, and assistant to the director, Off-Campus Credit Programs, Indiana University-Purdue University, Indianapolis, Indiana

Emma Lou Thornbrough, professor emeritus, Butler University, Indianapolis, Indiana

Stanley Warren, professor emeritus, DePauw University, Greencastle, Indiana

Education and Culture

More than a Church: The Educational Role of the African Methodist Episcopal Church in Indiana, 1844–1861

Lori B. Jacobi

Separate black churches first appeared in America at the end of the eighteenth century. These churches emerged as the free black population in the North faced discrimination in mixed churches and set out to establish churches of their own where they could be treated as equals and truly participate. The most important of the early black churches was the African Methodist Episcopal (AME) church, which first assembled in 1794 in Philadelphia.[1] The church was founded by Richard Allen, who was dissatisfied with the white Methodist church, a church that was clearly unwilling to address black problems and concerns. African Methodist Episcopal theology was based on Wesley's Methodism, but in the AME church theology was used to devise practical solutions to immediate physical and social problems.[2] The mission of the church included development of the mind and "elevation of the race" through education, temperance, good personal habits, and fulfillment of spiritual needs.[3]

Like other black churches, the AME church was fashioned after the white church but expanded its role "to include political and social, as well as religious concerns."[4] This was especially true in Ohio and Indiana, then considered the West, where a new brand of African Methodism emerged.[5] One of the most prominent features of this "new brand" of African Methodism was an active interest in education. While Richard Allen was committed to the establishment of schools, it was in the West where the first AME seminary, Union Seminary, which later became Wilberforce University, appeared.[6] In Indiana the church attempted to take an active interest in education. This can be observed in the activities and sentiments of the members of the Indiana Conference of the AME church, a district that included all of the state plus parts of Michigan, Wisconsin, Iowa, Illinois, and Minnesota.

The Indiana Conference of the AME church was established in 1840 by a resolution passed at the annual conference at Baltimore.[7] The conference was organized and its first annual meeting was held at Blue River, Indiana, on 2 October 1840.[8] This marked the culmination of years of work by the Reverend William Paul Quinn. Quinn was instrumental in establishing the Indiana conference and remained an important force in the region until his death in 1873. Little is known about his early life except that he was born in Calcutta, India, in 1788. He became a member of the AME church in Bucks County, Pennsylvania, in 1808 and was licensed to preach there in 1812. In 1833 Quinn was readmitted to the church after several years of separation, which was prompted by a disagreement with Bishop Allen.[9]

At the New York General Conference in 1833, Quinn was assigned to the Ohio Conference as an itinerant and became a special missionary to the states west of the Ohio River in 1840. This assignment took him to Indiana, where he found independent AME congregations organizing and where he established several churches himself.[10] By 1844 Quinn could proudly report that the region (Indiana and Illinois) had forty-seven churches with two thousand members, seven traveling elders, twenty traveling preachers, twenty-seven local preachers, fifty Sunday schools with two hundred teachers and two thousand scholars, seventeen camp meetings, and forty temperance societies.[11] As a reward for his accomplishments, Quinn was ordained a bishop in 1844.[12]

Indiana was fertile ground for the growth of African Methodism. Sharing its southern border with the South, Indiana during the antebellum period was a likely place for escaped or freed slaves to head. The state offered a new beginning for blacks, but Hoosiers did not always welcome blacks with open arms. Article 6 of the Northwest Ordinance of 1787 forbade slavery in the Indiana Territory, but many white Hoosiers were determined to have the article repealed.[13] A state law passed in 1831 required that blacks who emigrated to Indiana pay a five hundred dollar bond. Laws prohibiting whites from marrying persons one-eighth or more black were not repealed in Indiana until 1965.[14] Given this hostility toward them, many blacks established segregated and isolated communities where Baptist and AME churches often appeared. A classic example is the Beech Settlement in Rush County, established in 1828 by free blacks from North Carolina who traveled to Indiana with Quakers. Out of the settlement grew a Baptist church and the AME church where the Indiana conference was born.[15] Often, the communities grew up around a hospitable Quaker community, as was the case in Richmond.[16]

In the early years, some blacks did attend mixed churches, but separate black churches became increasingly more popular. As Emma Lou Thornbrough has observed, the "most important of these was the African Methodist Episcopal Church, which was a potent force not only in the religious life, but also in education and in the development of race pride and unity."[17] In Indianapolis, for example, Elder Moses Broyles, pastor of the Second Baptist Church, observed, "The Baptist Church had very little influence in the community. All religious influence was in the A.M.E. Church."[18]

The AME church in Indiana took its role seriously and, like its eastern counterparts, made every effort to play a broad role in the community. As a part of this role, the church took an active interest in furthering education for blacks. The cause of education was a recurring theme at the annual meetings of the Indiana Conference[19] and in articles by Hoosiers found in the *Repository of Religion and Literature and of Science and Art,* an official organ of the AME church literary societies, which was published in Indianapolis from 1858 to 1861.

The preachers of the Indiana Conference had great respect and hope for education. As Elisha Weaver, editor of the *Repository* during its Indiana years and pastor of the Bethel AME Church in Indianapolis, wrote,

> The road to honor and usefulness lies open to all who will obtain this knowledge. Why should we desire to possess this knowledge? . . . [To] better enable us to participate in the happiness and enjoy the beauty, order, and harmony of this beautiful creation, and open us to a wider sphere for usefulness; it will enable us to rend apart the darkening vail [*sic*] of bigotry and superstition; it will enable us to palliate the suffering and relieve the sorrows of our fellowmen.[20]

Such attitudes were translated into concerted efforts to establish Sabbath and day schools and a seminary in Indiana. In 1859 the *Repository* reported that the Indiana Conference had spent fourteen hundred dollars on education since 1851, an enormous sum, and an educational society was founded that year to raise money for schools. The society collected dues and solicited money from whites, who were reaping the benefits of black tax dollars that went to schools that blacks were not welcomed to attend.[21] In November 1858 Rev. Elisha Weaver advertised the "chance for a good education, in Indianapolis, Ind.," as he had

IHS

Bethel AME Church, a pioneer institution in Indianapolis, was a social, educational, and religious center for African-Americans dating from the antebellum period.

set up a boarding school at his church in Indianapolis. The school offered instruction in spelling, reading, writing, arithmetic, grammar, geography, history, anatomy, physiology, hygiene, and other subjects on "fair terms."[22]

Despite these achievements, the church in Indiana struggled in its educational endeavors. In the area of Sabbath schools, Reverend Quinn reported fifty with 2,000 "scholars" in 1844, while in 1856 Thomas Strother, William Dove, and William Jackson reported to the general conference that only 1,484 students were attending day and Sabbath schools combined.[23] Thus, there was a decline in students while membership in the church increased from 1,168 in 1840 to 1,369 in 1856.[24] The decline is even more significant considering that Quinn's 1844 statistics were for Indiana and Illinois, while the 1856 statistics were for the entire conference, which embraced portions of Michigan, Wisconsin, Iowa, Illinois, and Minnesota.[25] None of the other states of the Indiana Conference, however, contained substantial numbers of AME churches to warrant the creation of a separate conference during the antebellum period.

In an effort to explain this decline in students, it should be noted that there is some evidence that the people of Indiana were not satisfied with the progress of the Sabbath schools. In the November 1858 issue of the *Repository*, C. Jones Moore wrote from Indiana that more attention needed to be paid by the church to the "babes." Moore complained that, "We do not want to learn mere letters, for we can learn that at seminaries, &c, but it is religious instruction that is needed in the Sabbath Schools, and the ministers are the ones we look to for it."[26]

Similarly, in an article entitled "Are We Doing What We Can?," James Lynch of Indiana demanded more from the Sabbath school. Lynch observed that there was general agreement among the members of his church that "the hope of the colored people is in the rising generation," yet they had neglected the youth among them.[27] This neglect could do more damage to their cause "than that of the most favored class (whites)," and ministers, teachers, and parents alike were guilty.[28] Lynch continued his comments in the next issue of the *Repository,* concluding that no colored organization has the power to change youth like the African Methodist Episcopal Church. Lynch believed it was the responsibility of the church to develop the character of others.[29] These writings may very well represent hints of discontent in Indiana, but it is also possible that students were either attending schools not associated with the AME church or that the agricultural pursuits that engaged most of the state's black population did not allow time for regular attendance.

Along with the Sabbath schools, the Indiana Conference was concerned about educating the clergy in the West. Standards were set for new preachers and they had to be met. At the Indiana Conference in 1858 the committee on orders and admissions reported that candidates Hall, Strother, Trevan, Cain, Rush, and Nelson had been examined on the following: the second and third sections of the books of creeds, the duties of a deacon, church government, English grammar, geography, and arithmetic. All were found deficient in all areas. The committee also reported that "candidates for elders were also examined on the duties of elders and government and doctrine of the church and we find them very deficient in all of their studies except brother Strother, who is more advanced in his studies than others but deficient in church government."[30] The committee recommended that all candidates continue to study.[31]

The efforts of the Indiana Conference to establish a seminary were continually frustrated. The Reverend R. M. Johnson was appointed by the conference to raise money for its operation in the state. At the annual meeting in 1851, Johnson reported that he had been unsuccessful in his efforts to establish a seminary in Indiana. The biggest obstacles preventing Johnson from achieving his goal were the "black laws," which kept blacks from participating in the social and economic life of the state.[32] By 1855 the Indiana Conference had begun to explore other options outside the boundaries of its own state. At this time the education committee reported that the Cincinnati Conference of the Methodist Episcopal church had developed a proposal for the "moral, intellectual and religious elevation of the colored people of the United States."[33] The committee made two recommendations: that a committee be established to work with the Methodist Episcopal church and that active work continue in Indiana and Illinois to establish a seminary. Should these efforts fail, negotiations with the Methodist Episcopal Union Seminary in Ohio were recommended.[34]

An important figure in the push for a seminary and education in general in the West was Bishop Daniel Alexander Payne. Payne became a bishop in 1852 and was the presiding bishop over an area including the Indiana Conference from 1856 to 1860. He was dedicated to furthering education for blacks and knew very well the problem faced in setting up schools; Payne's own school in South Carolina was closed in 1835 by a law forbidding the teaching of blacks.[35] Payne took his crusade West in 1856 and found a more hospitable environment for education. At the Ohio Conference in 1844, a committee was set up to work toward the establishment of a seminary, and in 1856 its efforts paid off. In that year the Methodist Episcopal and AME conferences of Ohio became joint managers of the newly incorporated Wilberforce University. In 1863 Payne purchased the university from the Methodist Episcopal church and sold the Union Seminary property associated with it. The seminary students and personnel were incorporated into the university.[36] Judging from the conference minutes, the people of Indiana praised and dedicated themselves to Wilberforce University, and there just may not have been enough people or funds to support another institution in the West.[37]

Wilberforce and its associated Union Seminary were among the few alternatives for higher education for Indiana blacks. Within the state, there were at least two institutions that accepted blacks, neither of which was associated with the

Daniel A. Payne, *Recollections of Seventy Years*, 1888

Bishop Daniel Alexander Payne, 1811–1893

church. South Hanover College in Jefferson County sent a letter to the 1852 Indiana Conference announcing that "provisions had been made for the education of three colored youths in the state, free of charge."[38] Also, the Baptist Eleutherian College in Lancaster, Jefferson County, admitted black students. From 1849 to 1861, 225 pupils attended Eleutherian, and of these 50 to 60 were black. But the Lancaster community was one-half "mildly in favor of or wholly indifferent to the institution of human slavery," and the other half bitterly opposed it. Life at Eleutherian was not always pleasant for the black students. In 1850 the black dormitories were burned, and by 1861 all the black students had abandoned the institution.[39]

The AME church in Indiana made efforts to expand its role in the area of education, but these efforts were often frustrated. The report of the education committee at the 1858 meeting is especially telling; having little to report from Indiana, the report is purposely vague and focuses on the educational efforts of the AME church at large. Wilberforce in Ohio and Avery College in Pennsylvania, a black school established by Rev. Charles Avery (not associated with the AME church), are presented as examples of education in the West.[40]

But, schools were not the only means to educate and inform. While the AME Book Concern, established in 1817, was responsible for the publication of the *Discipline* and hymnbooks, the church published various periodicals as well. These provided an open forum for ideas, a place to advertise, and a place to rally support. In Indiana an effort was made to show support for the *Christian Recorder* and the *Repository of Religion and Literature and of Science and Art,* two AME periodicals. The *Christian Recorder,* published erratically beginning in 1841, fought to establish itself as an official church organ in its early years. The paper was established by a resolution passed at the 1836 annual conference. After a brief gap in publication, a young Elisha Weaver of Madison, Indiana, wrote a letter to the editor dated 4 September 1854. Weaver expressed his happiness in seeing the *Recorder* back in print and praised the new editor, J. P. Campbell, whom he had met at the annual conference in New York. Illustrating support for the *Recorder* in the Indiana Conference, Weaver wrote, "The following persons have paid for the *Recorder* in advance: Vivian Tuch, North Madison, Indiana; Caroline Williams, Madison; Anne Sterritt, Louisville, Kentucky. Each $1.50. I have also paid mine."[41]

A year later, Willis Revels, an Indianapolis preacher, assured the readers of the *Recorder* that in Indiana "we are not dead to the interest of the book concern and paper—we are endeavoring at this time to again inspire confidence in those who have lost and no sooner will this be done than all can be done that we desire."[42] These comments came in the postscript of a letter to the *Recorder* in which Revels reported on the 1855 Indiana Conference. It was at this conference that the desire was expressed to establish an "organ through which we can publish our thoughts, thus concentrating on our great work."[43] Evidently the representatives at the conference saw advantages in having an AME periodical based in Indiana. Basic among these advantages must have been timely delivery. In 1856 Elisha Weaver wrote to the *Recorder* to voice his opinion about an item that appeared in one of the several months-old issues that he received in one mailing.[44] The item that caught Weaver's eye was a proposal that the *Recorder* be suspended and a monthly magazine take its place. This he opposed on three counts: Weaver had convinced a considerable number of people to subscribe to the *Recorder* and had promised them that it was a dependable publication; he did not believe that a magazine would "serve our people for the present"; and since the general conference ordered the issuing of the *Recorder,* any decision to discontinue it should be made only by the general conference.[45] To an extent, Weaver got his way as the *Recorder* continued publication, although erratically. There was a big gap from mid-1856 until 1861 during which no issues were produced. The *Recorder* reappeared in 1861 with none other than Elisha

Weaver as its editor. But, a more impressive victory had been won for Indiana in the intervening years. The *Repository* began publishing in Indianapolis in 1858 with Weaver and six other AME preachers as its editors. It remained in the city until 1861.

The *Repository* was published under the auspices of the literary societies of the Baltimore, Indiana, and Missouri conferences. These societies were set up to oversee the literary activities of the conference and recommend a course of study for its members.[46] In Indiana the "Literary and Historical Society" was organized at the Indiana Conference in 1856.[47] Members were divided into three classes: Junior, those exhibiting little or no progress in English grammar, geography, arithmetic, the Creeds, and Thomas's *First Lessons in Etymology;* Middle, students showing "considerable progress in the above"; and Senior, those who have acquired a "liberal education."[48] In addition to recommending the subjects to be mastered in order to achieve each level, the society proposed a daily routine:

> It is a law of physiology that when the stomach is performing its functions, the brain must be at rest. Therefore the student should never engage in any kind of study after breakfast nor supper, till the end of three quarters of an hour, nor after dinner till one hour and a half. He who will observe this rule will find himself a healthier man and a more successful student,—provided he will also retire to bed at nine and rise at four, or at ten and rise at five A.M.[49]

A study schedule was set up for every day of the week with Saturday being "exclusively devoted to pulpit preparation."[50]

The society was thorough and strict in executing its educational role, and this is reflective of the dedication to education in Indiana. The attention paid to the Sunday schools, establishing a seminary and periodicals, along with the activities of the Literary and Historical Society, provide concrete evidence of the educational role that the AME church played in Indiana.

Although the educational efforts of the Indiana Conference were often frustrated, Indiana was a part of the pioneering endeavors of the AME church in the West that resulted in the founding of Wilberforce University. Like its eastern counterparts, the AME church in Indiana played an expanded role in the community that made it much more than a church.

NOTES

1. Carol V. R. George, *Segregated Sabbaths: Richard Allen and the Emergence of Independent Black Churches, 1760–1840* (New York: Oxford University Press, 1973), 49–50. The church had its roots in the Free African Society established by Allen in 1787. Ibid., 51.

2. Ibid., 54.

3. Rt. Rev. James A. Handy, *Scraps of African Methodist Episcopal History* (Philadelphia: AME Book Concern, [1902]; reprint, Ann Arbor: University Microfilms, 1974), 127–28.

4. Emma Jones Lapsansky, " 'Since They Got Those Separate Churches': Afro-Americans and Racism in Jacksonian Philadelphia," *American Quarterly* 32 (1980): 63.

5. Paul R. Griffin, "A Brief Account of the Development and Work of African Methodism in Ohio and Indiana, 1830–1865," *Black History News & Notes* (Nov. 1985): 6.

6. James H. Smith, D.D., *Vital Facts Concerning the African Methodist Episcopal Church* (Philadelphia: AME Book Concern of the AME Church, 1939), 128–29.

7. Handy, *Scraps of African Methodist Episcopal History,* 136.

8. Ibid., 138; "Beech Homecoming," *Black History News & Notes* (Oct. 1980): 1. Blue River is another name for the Beech Settlement. The AME church at Beech was known as Mt. Pleasant or Beech church and was founded in 1832.

9. Handy, *Scraps of African Methodist Episcopal History,* 108; Richard Wright, *Centennial Encyclopaedia of the African Methodist Episcopal Church* (Philadelphia: Book Concern of the AME Church, 1916; reprint, Ann Arbor: University Microfilms, 1977), 280–81.

10. Griffin, "A Brief Account of the Development and Work of African Methodism," 5. The pre-1840 churches are difficult to track but include Vincennes (1839), Richmond (1836), and Beech (1832).

11. For Elder Quinn's 1844 report on missionary work in the Far West, see Daniel Alexander Payne, *History of the African Methodist Episcopal Church* (Nashville, Tenn.: Publishing House of the AME Sunday School Union, 1891; reprint, New York: Arno Press, 1969), 170–71.

12. Charles S. Smith, *A History of the African Methodist Episcopal Church* (Philadelphia: Book Concern of the AME Church, 1922), 16.

13. Jacqueline Cortez, *Contributions in Black and Red: Local History of Negro Settlement in Southwestern Indiana and Illinois* (Vincennes: Vincennes University Printing Center, 1976), 4–6.

14. Ibid., 1; Coy D. Robbins, "Miscegenation in Black History," *Black History News & Notes* (May 1981): 3.

15. "Beech Homecoming," 1; *Rush County Sesquicentennial Edition History, 1822–1972* (Rushville: Rush County Sesquicentennial, Inc., 1972), 17–18.

16. Emma Lou Thornbrough, *The Negro in Indiana before 1900: A Study of a Minority,* vol. 37 of *Indiana Historical Collections* (Indianapolis: Indiana Historical Bureau, 1957), 48.

17. Ibid., 151.

18. Elder Moses Broyles, *The History of the Second Baptist Church of Indianapolis* (Indianapolis: Printing and Publishing House Print, 1876), 28.

19. Notes concerning education from the annual meetings appear in the following: 1840—Smith, *Vital Facts,* 16, and Payne, *History,* 130; 1841—Smith, *Vital Facts,* 16, and Payne, *History,* 137; 1843—Payne, *History,* 180; 1851—ibid., 206; 1855—ibid., 327, and Bishop Daniel Alexander Payne, *Recollections of Seventy Years,* comp. Sarah C. Bierce Scarborough, ed. Rev. C. S. Smith (Nashville, Tenn.: Publishing House of the AME Sunday School Union, 1888; reprint, New York: Arno Press, 1968), 130; 1856—Payne, *History,* 405; "Conference Minutes, Indiana Conference, African Methodist Episcopal Church" (19th Annual Conference of the Indiana District, 1858), pp. 1–26, Benjamin Arnett Papers #35, Stokes Learning Resources Center Archives, Wilberforce University, Wilberforce, Ohio.

20. Elisha Weaver, "Knowledge," *Repository of Religion and Literature and of Science and Art* 1 (Apr. 1858): 39.

21. "Progress of Education in Indianapolis," ibid. 2 (July 1859): 132.

22. "Notice," ibid. 1 (Nov. 1858): 192.

23. Quinn's report in Payne, *History,* 170–71; education committee report of 1856 in ibid., 405. Quinn's statistics must be viewed with some skepticism. Given the growth of the black population in Indiana, one would expect the 1856 statistics to be larger. Census data reveal that the free colored population of the state increased from 7,168 in 1840 to 11,262 in 1850 to 11,428 in 1860. Growth was slowed after 1850 as a result of the fugitive slave law of that year and the 1851 Indiana Constitution.

24. Ibid., 130; Handy, *Scraps of African Methodist Episcopal History,* 221.

25. Griffin, "A Brief Account of the Development and Work of African Methodism," 6; Wright, *Centennial Encyclopaedia,* 372–74.

26. C. Jones Moore, "Sabbath Schools," *Repository of Religion and Literature and of Science and Art* 1 (Nov. 1858): 156.

27. James Lynch, "Are We Doing What We Can?," ibid. 2 (Apr.–July 1859): 59.

28. Ibid., 59–60.

29. Ibid., 105.

30. "Conference Minutes, 1858," p. 19.

31. Ibid., 20.

32. Payne, *History,* 260.

33. Ibid., 124.

34. Ibid., 326.

35. Ibid., 19–40.

36. Wright, *Centennial Encyclopaedia,* 372–74.

37. "Conference Minutes, 1858," p. 20.

38. Payne, *History,* 204. According to Broyles, Hanover was also known as College Hill.

39. Curtis Marshall, "Eleutherian College," *Indiana History Bulletin* 25 (Nov. 1948): 200–203.

40. "Conference Minutes, 1858," p. 20.
41. *The Christian Recorder,* 16 Sept. 1854, p. 77.
42. Ibid., 20 Oct. 1855, p. 35.
43. Payne, *History,* 326.
44. *The Christian Recorder,* 18 Jan. 1856, p. 151.
45. Ibid.
46. "Conference Minutes, 1858," p. 24.
47. Payne, *History,* 402.
48. "Conference Minutes, 1858," p. 24. The reference to Thomas's *First Lessons in Etymology* is probably Joseph Thomas's *The First Book of Etymology.*
49. "Conference Minutes, 1858," p. 26.
50. Ibid., 25.

Rev. John H. Clay and the 1879 Black Exodus to Greencastle, Indiana: A Case Study of AME Church Leadership

Arnold Cooper

The purpose of this study is to reconstruct and examine the role of John Henry Clay, an African Methodist Episcopal (AME) minister who served in west-central Indiana from 1878 to 1881 during a period of dramatic black migration to rural Indiana. As a case study, this inquiry into black ministerial leadership seeks to reclaim from the "shadow of neglect" an example of black Hoosier enterprise and activism.[1]

Born a slave in Oglethorpe County, Georgia, in 1851, Clay became a fugitive during the Civil War and gained the favor of a captain of an Indiana regiment. He and a companion were given the choice of coming north to Indianapolis when the Indiana soldier mustered out or remaining in the South. Clay was smuggled across the Ohio River, after reaching Louisville, to evade the Indiana law prohibiting the entry of blacks into the state. Befriended by a black music teacher, Clay went to school in Indianapolis and became a preacher in 1875. He served a church in Corydon (Harrison County) until he came to Greencastle in Putnam County three years later.[2]

The church that Clay came to serve in Greencastle was started by Luke and Charity Townsend, the first black residents of Putnam County. Luke came to Indiana in 1832 with his former master, James Townsend, who had emancipated his slaves in Kentucky. Townsend made Luke part of his household and gave him the family name. Described by a contemporary as "deeply religious," Luke helped start the first Sunday school in Putnamville with three young white friends. In the early 1840s Luke married a black woman named Charity, who had escaped injury when a slave trader's wagon overturned crossing Deer Creek on the National Road east of Putnamville. Benjamin Jones, a local farmer, purchased her freedom and took her into his home to help his wife. Luke and Charity, forever referred to as the "first colored people to locate in Putnam county," initially made their home in Putnamville, but eventually moved to Greencastle Junction (now Limedale) and raised eleven children.[3]

Sometime in the 1870s Luke died, and Charity was listed in the 1880 census as a widow with three children still at home.[4] During their marriage, the Townsends witnessed a significant increase in the number of blacks who resided in Putnam County. There were 34 black residents in 1850, but the number tripled to 105 by 1870. Most black Putnam County contemporaries were laborers, domestic servants, and farmers. A few blacks worked as barbers, carpenters, and cooks.[5]

Luke and Charity Townsend first joined Simpson Chapel, one of two white Methodist Episcopal churches in Greencastle, but decided to organize a "Methodist Mission" for blacks in their home in 1872. A granddaughter remembered that "Luke's strong bass voice could usually be heard above all others at their revival meetings." Membership reached thirteen a year later.[6] When the Indiana Conference of the AME Church met in 1875,

Indianapolis World, 13 February 1892

The only known picture of Rev. John H. Clay

the congregation that the Townsends had started joined similar efforts in nearby Brazil and Plainfield as part of the "Greencastle Mission." An "itinerant deacon" was appointed in 1876 to shepherd the affairs of these churches.[7]

As membership increased, the congregation of the Methodist Mission moved from the Townsends' home to a room above a store on the courthouse square in Greencastle. Church services did not go unnoticed by the local press. When the "colored brethren" hold a revival at the room in Albin's block, "their singing attracts crowds of white people, who listen with much interest to the quaint religious songs." Meetings at Albin's Hall garnered "considerable attention from outsiders."[8]

When Clay arrived in Greencastle, he was determined to build a church for his congregation of forty-three, and he used the local media to state his objective. He addressed local citizens in April 1878 through an "Appeal from the A.M.E. Church of

Greencastle," stating his intent to "canvass the city" and "call on every one to assist us in this worthy enterprise." He minced no words: "The condition of the colored people of Greencastle is bad. They are without a church building in which to worship God, and in which to hold Sabbath-school." Clay planned monthly concerts with admission fees of ten and fifteen cents to raise money for lumber.[9]

Success did not elude Clay's efforts. By December 1878, instead of building a new structure, the congregation purchased St. Benedict's Roman Catholic Church for one thousand dollars with an initial payment of two hundred dollars. The congregation planned to put on a new roof, repaint the building, and "papered within and otherwise put [the church] in good shape."[10] The church was ready for occupancy ten days before Christmas. Jubilation reigned: "Every one present seemed to be in a joyful mood. They felt that they were in their own house." A local paper described Clay as "an honest man [who] is doing a good work. His concert troupe will continue to give entertainments for the benefit of the church. All who hear them are greatly pleased."[11]

An admiring black newspaper believed that Clay was a "living demonstration of the boundless possibilities of an energetic Afro-American."[12] A further example of Clay's ministerial activism involved the 1879 exodus of blacks from North Carolina to Indiana. A combination of political disfranchisement, economic destitution, and the abridgment of civil rights precipitated an exodus from the South in 1879. While Kansas became a principal destination, migration to Indiana also swelled because of promoters promising work as farm laborers.[13] Two blacks from North Carolina, Samuel Perry and Peter Williams, traveled to Indianapolis in mid-1879 to investigate the possibilities of bringing a contingent of their Tar Heel neighbors to the state. Perry also visited George Langsdale, white editor of the *Greencastle Banner* who had promoted migration in his newspaper, and Clay, who had authored a circular printed in the *Banner* encouraging blacks to settle in Indiana.[14]

Langsdale, a native of Indianapolis, served in the Civil War, purchased the *Banner* in 1868, and became influential enough in the Republican party to be appointed postmaster of Greencastle in 1874 and 1878.[15] Langsdale testified before a United States Senate investigation of the migration that he "saw no impropriety in the colored people of the South coming to the North. . . . For some time the conviction had been growing on me that the only thing the late slaves could do to become men in the true sense of the word, would be for them to come to the North."[16]

Clay aligned himself with Langsdale and played a significant role in advertising the benefits of black migration. The black minister described his adopted state in a circular printed in July 1879 as a "state of fertile lands, with abundant timber of every variety. The climate is healthful and is not too cold for me, although I was raised in Georgia." Black migrants would discover "free schools are maintained from three to six months each year in every neighborhood," and that plenty of employment opportunities awaited their arrival. Clay cautioned that "what we want is honest, industrious men, who know how and are willing to work on farms, and the same class of women to do housework. Loafers are not wanted."[17]

Clay's appeal did not neglect political considerations. He asserted that "in Indiana all stand equal before the law—the black man being protected in his contracts, property, and person the same as the white." As a fugitive slave, Clay urged blacks to "gather up what you have and come at once, so as to be safe when the fifteenth amendment is repealed, for the purpose of returning you to a condition of slavery, if you are found south of the Ohio river." He exhorted blacks to "hitch up your teams and come overland to Indiana, like the children of Israel marched out of Egypt."[18]

Clay's activism included more than writing a circular. He played an active role when approximately 250 blacks from North Carolina settled in Greencastle between November 1879 and January 1880. When the first group of 56 migrants arrived in November, Clay met them at the railroad depot and "marched them up to the church and quartered them there."[19] Bethel Chapel, the name of Clay's church, became a reception center and a social service enterprise for the new black residents. This was not the first occasion that Clay had used his church to welcome and assist migrants. When a party of "colored refugees" from Kentucky passed through Greencastle on their way to Kansas in September 1879, they were "taken in charge by Rev. J. H. Clay and his congregation and entertained in Bethel Chapel."[20]

Migrants to Greencastle and local officials both acknowledged Clay's leadership. James A. Stokes, a migrant from Rocky Mount, North Carolina, testified that Clay found him a job in a nearby community. Another migrant arrived in a mail car carrying a paper directing him to see Clay upon arrival.[21] One migrant, Charles Woods, who was five years old when he arrived with his family, remembered the reception at the train station: "We were met at the station by a committee of colored folks headed by the pastor of the AME church. We were taken to the church where refreshments were provided by the good people of the town."[22] When a contingent of new arrivals wanted to use the courthouse to hold a meeting to explain why they had come to Greencastle, the local sheriff told the group that Clay would have to vouch for them before permission would be granted.[23]

Clay's solicitude of and sustenance for the migrants who came to Greencastle can be explained from several perspectives. First, he followed in the steps of other AME ministers who supported southern black migration to their communities. J. H. Walker, an AME minister in nearby Terre Haute, encouraged the Emigrant Aid Society of Washington, D. C., to send migrants to work in the coal mines.[24] Black churches in Indianapolis formed the Christian Emigrant Aid Society to help meet the needs of new arrivals. The Vermont Street AME Church and the Second Baptist Church had their own relief societies.[25]

Clay's active involvement in the migration to Indiana also corresponded with the stance of the Indiana Conference of the

LIST OF APPOINTMENTS.

STATIONS.	MINISTERS.	NO.
Richmond	W. R. Kevels	1
Bethel, Indianapolis	James M. Townsend	2
Allen Chapel, "	W. S. Lankford	3
Bethel, Detroit	Johnson Mitchem	4
Ebenezer, "	Robinson Jeffries	5
Evansville	Morris Lewis	6
Terre Haute	A. T. Hall	7
New Albany	Richard Titus	8
Vincennes	H. H. Wilson	9
Ypsilanti	Jason Bundy	10
Crawfordsville	Jessse Bass	11
Mt. Vernon	Martin Coleman	12

CIRCUITS.	NAMES.	
Charleston	James Simpson	1
New Garden	John Furguson	2
Mitchell	A. H. Knight	3
Knightstown	C. H. Gilmore	4
Cambridge City	J. H. Alexander	5
Lafayette	Mattison Patterson	6
Logansport	H. H. Thompson	7
Kalamazoo	John McSmith	8
Franklin	Alexander Smith	9
Madison	George Chavous	10
Rockville	Johnson Burden	11
Brownsville	A. J. Furguson	12
Ann Arbor	H. B. Gordon	13
St. Joseph	J. Jordan	14
Princeton	Henry Harper	15
Muncie	L. D. Crosby	16
Greencastle	J. H. Clay	17
South Bend	Peter Davis	18
Saginaw	John Myers	19

MISSIONS.	NAMES.	
Marion	Richard Hutchinson	1
Indianapolis Mission	George B. Pope	2
Pontiac	J. J. Crow	3
Corydon	Louis Ratliff	4
Marshall	J. P. Coates	5
Grand Rapids	John W. Harper	6
Fort Wayne	George O. Curtis	7
Total		38

List of appointments included in the Proceedings of the 38th [1877] Annual Session of the Indiana Conference of the African Methodist Episcopal Church Held at Bethel Church in Indianapolis.

AME Church. Delegates to the Fortieth Session (1879) praised the "noble and generous hearted citizens of Kansas and other states in the west [who] have given [the migrants] not only homes in their rich and fertile territories, but food, shelter and protection for their destitute families."[26] Clay and his church thus became part of the AME connection that operated in several states. An AME minister from North Carolina, who supported migration to the Midwest, "stopped at points having similar churches, to whose pastors he confided his mission." Black migrants found their way to communities west of Indianapolis "through the medium of the colored churches. Mr. Williams [Rev. P. C. Williams, an AME minister], for illustration, visited this city [Greencastle] and interested the pastor and members of the church here." A local newspaper recognized that "Rev. John H. Clay, pastor of the colored church, has stood at the wheel and guided the affair."[27]

Clay's relationship to the black exodus stemmed not only from his position as an AME minister, but also as a fugitive slave who knew the travail of bondage. He understood the life experiences of migrants who brought a legacy of servitude with them. Clay could, no doubt, discern in a special way the testimony of Spear Pitman, one of his parishioners, who came to Greencastle from North Carolina in 1880. Pitman stated that "every year I was put up on the block and auctioned off to work for a year for some other plantation owner, whoever bid the most got me for a year. . . . The bad ones whipped for nothing at all, lots of times. Whenever they would get on a strain about something, they would whip us to work it off."[28]

As a minister, Clay provided temporal and spiritual support for the migrants. Consonant with the mission of his denomination, he envisioned the black exodus to his community as an opportunity for black people to improve their economic and social position.[29] Bethel Chapel became a welcome center for "kindred—bound to us by the strongest ties that bind men together." A dispatch from Greencastle to a black weekly noted that the migrants could now "breathe the air of freedom for the first time in their lives."[30] Clay galvanized support for the new arrivals. He adeptly used the local media and formed a useful alliance with the white editor of the local Greencastle newspaper. He skillfully operated within the structure of the AME church connection.

Clay left Greencastle in 1881 for subsequent assignments in Bloomington, Terre Haute, and New Albany before he became pastor of Bethel AME Church in Indianapolis (1888), the largest black congregation in Indiana.[31] He died at the age of forty-one in 1892, leaving behind a legacy in Greencastle that was a call to the survival of his people.

Notes

1. Albert J. Raboteau and David W. Wills, "Retelling Carter Woodson's Story: Archival Sources for Afro-American Church History," *Journal of American History* 77 (June 1990): 185.

2. *Indianapolis World,* 10 May 1890.

3. Jesse W. Weik, *Weik's History of Putnam County, Indiana* (Indianapolis: B. F. Bowen & Co., 1910), 200; *Greencastle Herald Democrat,* 4 June 1915; Clifton Phillips, "Putnam County Blacks in the 19th Century" (Mimeographed copy in possession of the author). A personal account of Luke and Charity is found in Christine Collins, "The Story of Luke Townsend" (Mimeographed copy in possession of the author). Collins was a confidant of Agnes James Richard, a granddaughter of the Townsends, who told the story of her grandparents to Collins. Contemporary recollections of the Townsend family can be found in the "Oral History of the Black Community in Greencastle, Indiana," three tapes #736, DePauw University Archives, Greencastle, Ind.

4. United States Census Office, *Tenth Census of the United States, 1880: Population Schedules, Putnam County, Indiana,* microfilm, DePauw University Archives.

5. United States Census Office, *Seventh Census, 1850: Report of the United States* (Washington, D.C.: Robert Armstrong, 1853), 773; United States Census Office, *Eleventh Census, 1890: Population,* 15 vols. (Washington, D.C.: Government Printing Office, 1895), 1:409.

6. Clifton Phillips, ed., *From Frontier Circuit to Urban Church: A History of Greencastle Methodism* (Greencastle, Ind.: Gobin Memorial United Methodist Church, 1989), 18, 61; Collins, "The Story of Luke Townsend," 1; *Atlas of Putnam County, Indiana* (Chicago: J. H. Beers & Co., 1879), 8.

7. *Thirty-Sixth Annual Conference of the African Methodist Episcopal Church for the Indiana District,* held at Detroit, Michigan, 26 Aug.–1 Sept. 1875 (Richmond, Ind.: Free Press Stam Printing House, 1875), 18; Benjamin Arnett Papers #35, Stokes Learning Resources Center Archives, Wilberforce University, Wilberforce, Ohio; *Minutes of the*

Thirty-Seventh Session of the Indiana Annual Conference of the A. M. E. Church, held at Hill's Chapel, Grant County, Indiana, 24–29 Aug. 1876 (Terre Haute, Ind.: The Globe Book Bindery, 1876), 2, 33, 27; Arnett Papers #35.

8. *Greencastle Banner,* 29 Feb. and 9 Aug. 1877.

9. Ibid., 21 Mar., 17 Oct., and 11 Apr. 1878.

10. Ibid., 5 Dec. 1878; *Atlas of Putnam County, Indiana,* 8.

11. *Greencastle Banner,* 19 Dec. 1878.

12. *Indianapolis World,* 10 May 1890.

13. Nell Irvin Painter, *The Exodusters: Black Migration to Kansas after Reconstruction* (New York: Knopf, 1977); Emma Lou Thornbrough, *The Negro in Indiana before 1900: A Study of a Minority,* vol. 37 of *Indiana Historical Collections* (Indianapolis: Indiana Historical Bureau, 1957), 120, 31, 58.

14. Thornbrough, *The Negro in Indiana,* 216–18.

15. *Atlas of Putnam County, Indiana,* 42.

16. *Report and Testimony of the Select Committee of the United States Senate to Investigate the Causes of the Removal of the Negroes from the Southern States to the Northern States,* Senate Reports, 46th Cong., 2d sess., No. 693 in three parts (Washington, D.C.: Government Printing Office, 1880), 2:508.

17. Ibid., 1:166.

18. Ibid.

19. Ibid., 174.

20. Ibid., 167; Thornbrough, *The Negro in Indiana,* 224.

21. *Report of the Removal of the Negroes,* 2:319–20, 1:328.

22. *Greencastle Banner,* n.d.

23. *Report of the Removal of the Negroes,* 1:179.

24. Ibid., 1:18, 92.

25. Ibid., 1:355, 356.

26. *Minutes of the Fortieth Session of the Indiana Annual Conference of the African Methodist Episcopal Church,* held at Ypsilanti, Michigan, 21–27 Aug. 1879 (Richmond, Ind.: Daily Palladium Steam Printing Establishment, 1879), 18–19; Arnett Papers #35.

27. *Greencastle Banner,* 8 Jan. 1880.

28. WPA Files: Putnam County 267.5 (Slave Narratives), Indiana State University, Rare Books Department, Cunningham Memorial Library, Terre Haute, Indiana.

29. Clarence E. Walker, *A Rock in a Weary Land: The African Methodist Episcopal Church during the Civil War and Reconstruction* (Baton Rouge: Louisiana State University Press, 1982), 2.

30. *Indianapolis Leader,* 6 Dec. 1879.

31. *Indianapolis World,* 13 Feb. 1892.

The Evolution of Secondary Schooling for Blacks in Indianapolis, 1869–1930

Stanley Warren

The education of blacks, particularly in the North during the late nineteenth and early twentieth centuries, did not always follow the traditions of time and place. Several northern states had developed public school systems by the beginning of the Civil War, but, more often than not, had no formal arrangement for the education of blacks. Even so, many classrooms were sparsely dotted with black students because some communities were so thinly populated with blacks that segregation was not feasible. This was the case in Indiana where the public schools, early in the postbellum period, were reestablished after undergoing a severe financial crisis. In 1869 the last barrier for black students was hurdled when the Indiana legislature legalized entry by blacks into the public education system.[1] Not surprisingly, local translations of the law led to separate elementary schools for blacks. Additionally, a new school law passed in 1877 stated that if no local facility existed for black students, they could attend schools designated for whites.[2]

Seldom was there an immediate bifurcation of the education system into black and white; instead, situations in individual communities dictated the extent of separation of races in the schools. A notable exception was Gary, Indiana, where segregation was introduced in the earliest years of the school system as part of William Wirt's "Gary Plan." The 1908 segregation plan concocted for thirty-three black elementary pupils segregated schools in Gary by administrative sanction until residential patterns made the issue of school integration a moot point.[3]

A contributing factor to the increasing educational demands by blacks was the growth of industrialization in specific northern cities and the arrival of poorly educated blacks from the South. In 1930 there were twenty-five northern cities, including Indianapolis and Gary, with black populations in excess of ten thousand.[4] This accounted for over 1.5 million blacks who had migrated northward in varying degrees since before the turn of the century. Some came with the idea that education was a necessity for a "better life," and others soon caught the fever.

Originally, it was felt that most blacks would not pursue education beyond the elementary level since there were no mandatory education laws nor were there great expectations for blacks to become educated except from their own families and communities. However, by 1920 nearly eight hundred black students were enrolled at Emmerich Manual, Arsenal Technical, and Shortridge high schools in Indianapolis, although they were far from being part of the fabric of these predominantly white institutions. Team sports and club activities were traditionally segregated, and that led some teachers to require segregated seating in their classrooms. Even so, there is evidence that many black students were learning a great deal. Much to the chagrin of those who felt that blacks were out of place, in 1915 Merle Stokes missed being number one in her graduating class at Shortridge High School by thirty-seven hundredths of a point.[5] This is only one of several success stories emanating from this arrangement; a situation which, no doubt, encouraged some adults in the black community to accept this spurious status accorded their children.

Although there may have been some white student and staff dissatisfaction about black students being in the schools, the lines had been drawn, and most seemed willing to allow the status quo to remain, but for the intrusion of outside forces. Civic groups, local government officials, and a growing desire to retain traditional housing patterns seemed to arrive at a point in time that would not allow this arrangement to continue. The inclusion of schools in complaints about integrated neighborhoods in the 1920s made it impossible to separate the development of black secondary schools in Indianapolis from the pressures on residential patterns in the city. Blacks were in pursuit of better housing that led them to "white" neighborhoods. They seemed perfectly satisfied that their younger children were attending racially segregated elementary schools but, because no black school existed beyond the elementary level, their older children were enrolled in racially mixed high schools. While there was little pressure from blacks to change the situation, whites were fearful that these "intruders" were about to overrun their neighborhoods and their schools.

There were several incidences of black families trying to move into "forbidden territory." One situation in particular alarmed the white community. Lucian Meriwether, a local dentist, attempted to emulate the American dream by purchasing a home in a near-northside area of the city in 1921. The move, seemingly simple on its face, was another thorn in the side of the Capitol Avenue Protective Association. The association, along with several other protesters appearing before the local school board, dedicated itself to preventing blacks from just such northward movement. In the minds of the public there existed a white and a black section of the city; although the boundaries were not marked, they were certainly real. Neighbors on both sides of Meriwether objected so strenuously to his presence that they installed six-foot-high wooden fences between their homes and his. These "spite fences," as they were called by a local newspaper, were the basis for a $10,000 damage

IHS C2244

IHS C2245

Students at School No. 24 plant a garden in 1908 and engage in a 1909 May Day celebration.

IHS C2172

Laura J. Wolfolk instructs an eighth-grade boys cooking class at School No. 26 in 1921.

suit filed by attorney Robert L. Bailey on behalf of Meriwether. Removal of the fences and the $500 judgment in favor of the plaintiff, although far short of the original amount sought, marked a high point in the attempts by blacks to push aside white constraints.[6] Unfortunately, this victory, which must have seemed so very significant at the time, was to have little lasting impact. Several other local associations were moving in a direction similar to that of the Capitol Avenue Protective Association, and the result was a new assault on the liberties of black citizens.

A number of public writers and historians seem convinced that the Ku Klux Klan was not a major factor in the growth of education-related prejudice and acts of racism in Indiana in the 1920s. It seems reasonable, however, that the atmosphere stemming from Klan activities was ideally suited to the growth of overt racism by neighborhood associations. It is an indisputable fact that much of the progress toward segregating high school students occurred during the time when the Klan was making an indelible political imprint on the city and state. A growing black population and the futility of trying to contain blacks within certain communities added to the difficulties.[7] Although "integrated" education at the secondary level in Indianapolis and the enrollment of a few black students in white elementary schools existed, the forces of segregation continued to exert a powerful influence over the city. Growing dissatisfaction coincided with the increasing influence of the Klan, whose membership had spread like tentacles throughout the most powerful social, civic, and business organizations in the state. The cry for segregated high schools was not localized nor was it confined to a single organization; the statewide movement, like a tide washing over the land, became politically and socially popular with people from all walks of life.

With one notable exception, the Klan kept a low profile where individual schools were concerned. Even though it was integrated, local Klansmen seemed particularly fond of Arsenal Technical High School. Often there were editorials about the school in *The Fiery Cross,* containing statements such as: "With our wonderful Arsenal Technical High School sending our Indianapolis boys 'on to Butler [University],' we have faith in the future of our state, and with a reorganization of the Indianapolis School Board being forced we have hope for our city schools."[8] The irony of Klan support for education became even more pronounced when the organization began lobbying for a Federal Department of Education with cabinet-level status.[9]

Mounting interest in the creation of a separate high school for black students seems to have been undergirded by a series of letters to, and appearances before, the school board. With few exceptions, black citizens protested the move and whites supported it. Fear among blacks was a constant factor as the strength of those favoring the separatist movement continued to grow. A call for membership in the female-dominated White Supremacy League echoed this point: "The league is in need of some big, red-blooded all white gentlemen to serve on its board. . . . We already have lawyers, merchants, court judges, governors, United States and State senators."[10] In a letter to W. E. B. Du Bois, a concerned Indianapolis citizen described the beginnings of this self-acknowledged racist organization. According to the letter, the organization was started by an Indianapolis woman on West Maple Road (38th Street), 5 July 1922. Its constitution included supremacy of the white race in all government offices, separate schools, no political association of blacks and whites, and isolation of whites who associate with "Negroes."[11]

After the Meriwether case, escalation of plans to separate high school students by race was the order of the day. At meetings in November and December 1922 letters from various groups regarding plans to erect a separate high school for black students were presented to the school board. The development of this grass-roots movement seemed to grow undisturbed by the "Garveyesque" notions about separatism and colonization that were popular in black communities on the East Coast and, to some extent, the West Coast. The bulk of the letters from blacks protesting the move included those from local doctors, lawyers, and ministers. One letter of protest, indicating that the proposal was "unchristian, anti-social, divisive in spirit, and pernicious," was illustrative of a large block of community sentiment. It was signed by members of a local civic group, the Better Indianapolis League, which included attorney and legislator Robert Brokenburr and Lionel Artis, public housing administrator.[12] Generally, the letters offered no alternatives; the protesters seemed more interested in maintaining the status quo than in bringing about change.

An accommodationist stance by blacks, according to Judy Jolley Mohraz in *The Separate Problem,* failed to stem the tide of white reaction and racism in Indianapolis just as it did in Chicago, where there was a significant degree of political power and militancy in the black community.[13] It is more likely that black citizens in Indianapolis were similar to those depicted in *The Paradox of Progressive Education:* "No clear consensus existed within the black community as to what should be accomplished. Blacks were particularly torn between advocating integration in principle and accepting separation in practice."[14]

However, it appears the protest letters were too little and too late. The next order of business at the December 1922 school board meeting, immediately after some of the letters were presented, was consideration of the proposal to build a new high school exclusively for black students. In a somewhat upbeat, positive statement (an attempt to show this move as best for the black community), the board approved the measure unanimously. Seeds of the idea that a new high school for black students would mean more jobs for black teachers were also planted at the meeting.[15] Once the statement was released and it became apparent that blacks in Indianapolis and from around the state were going to resist the move toward a separate high school, support for the plan from interested white factions increased. Shortly thereafter, a letter from the president of the White Supremacy League, who also claimed to represent a northside group called the Mapleton Civic Organization, was received by the board requesting separate schools for "Negro" children. Officers of the league addressed the board in an attempt to press home the point. Before officially accepting their letter, board president Charles Barry filed a disclaimer stating that the letter contained such statements that it could not be properly received without reservation and assurance that the board was not endorsing the position taken by the organization.[16] A representative of the Federation of Civic Clubs presented a resolution stating that one-fourth of city deaths were black; incurable consumption was creating great social needs among the black population; housing conditions were congested; and there were large numbers of black children in the schools in the insipient stages of tuberculosis. The final blow emanating from this amalgam of "evidence" was a recommendation from the federation that there should be separate black schools and teachers as well as separate facilities at Sunnyside Sanitarium for black tuberculosis patients.[17] The thrust of this resolution indicated that the organization was well aware of some of the health and socioeconomic considerations gripping the black community; yet their greatest concern was to achieve full separation of the races.

Later in the same year, G. A. Millett, chairman of the subcommittee of the Committee on Education of the Indianapolis Chamber of Commerce, addressed the board with a renewed request for a separate black high school. Millett urged George Buck, principal of Shortridge High School, to speak. Buck, as expected, echoed Millett's sentiments.[18] Shortly afterwards, a bond issue of $1,638,772 was recommended; this included sites and alterations for a black high school, a west side high school, and a black elementary school.[19] The stage was set for a dramatic population shift in the Indianapolis public schools.

From the beginning, the proposed new black school, which was to become Crispus Attucks High School, was plagued with uncertainty. The idea of placing it next to Public School 17 on West Street, with accommodations for one thousand students, received a negative vote from commissioner Bert Gadd, while commissioners Charles Barry and William Allison did not vote on the measure. A plan to select architects received two negative votes from Barry and Allison. Barry objected to some of the moves being made because a new board was to be seated on 1 January 1924.[20] Barry's misgivings may have centered on the enormity of the projects being considered at that time. In addition to the new black high school and the west side high school (Washington), a new Shortridge High School and expansion of the elementary schools were being planned. Although property upon which the black high school was to be built had been listed for taxation, including improvements, at $32,930, it was appraised for the board at a significantly higher $51,510 and offered to them for an even higher $62,975.[21]

Many black citizens were unhappy that their children were unable to attend Public School 36, which was near their homes but happened to be located on North Capitol Avenue in an area designated as "white" territory. Archie Greathouse, a local black resident, filed a suit to have children from the area who had been transferred some distance southward to Public School 42 returned to School 36. Greathouse also filed a separate suit in an attempt to halt construction of the proposed black high school. Although site purchases and construction were halted for a time, the cases were eventually decided against Greathouse.[22] In a display of either humor or bitterness, someone had written in the board minutes: "Mr. Greathouse has time in which to file a million complaints." This was changed to read, "an amended complaint."[23] Knowing that 15 July 1925 was a target date for having alleys and structures vacated and grounds cleared, the board, confident that the city government was behind it and that the Greathouse matter was no longer of any consequence, proceeded with business as planned, in spite of objections from W. E. Henderson, attorney for Greathouse.[24]

A series of letters between Walter White, assistant secretary of the NAACP, and W. S. Henry, a local attorney, reveals that beneath the surface side issues may have captured some of the attention of lawyers involved in the Greathouse case. The national office of the NAACP considered the brief in the case to block the creation of the Jim Crow high school to be very weak, and attempts were made to secure the services of additional counsel from one of the local white law firms. Relations between W. E. Henderson, W. S. Henry, and R. L. Bailey, local black attorneys representing the Indianapolis branch of the NAACP, and the national office of the NAACP grew worse following accusations that the attorneys assigned to the case were seeking "very high fees." After F. B. Ransom, attorney for the Madam C. J. Walker Company, reputedly told Walter White that not one of the three lawyers involved was competent to handle the case properly, the national office withdrew from the case. Soon afterward, during the residential segregation case of 1926, the three attorneys temporarily associated themselves with a local white firm.[25]

An *Indianapolis Star* article about plans to build the new "Negro" schools caused the PTA of School 69 to respond with the following letter: "May we earnestly petition the board to do all in their power to keep these schools south of 25th Street; [*sic*] nearest 21st Street. A colored park and a colored orphan's home has [*sic*] been pushed into white territory. Therefore, as taxpayers and citizens, we again ask the board to place the colored schools in colored territory. . . . Do we not as white citizens and taxpayers deserve as safe and healthful a school as the colored of the city. . . . A white high school is to be erected at a cost of $400,000; a colored at $550,000."[26] With the Greathouse case out of the way and with approval of the board attorney,

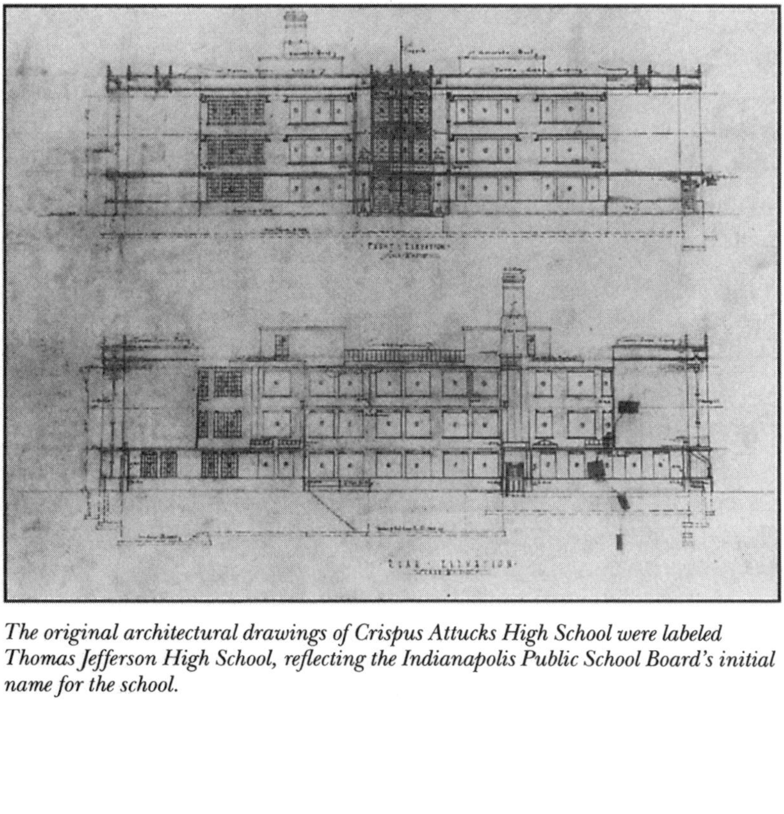

IHS C4254

The original architectural drawings of Crispus Attucks High School were labeled Thomas Jefferson High School, reflecting the Indianapolis Public School Board's initial name for the school.

work on the plan for a new black high school progressed. Bids on property were received and an auction of items on the land was held. The auctioneer was none other than the well-known Democrat, Indianapolis Mayor Samuel Lewis Shank.[27]

Symptomatic of the lack of understanding by the board or the lack of regard for blacks was the process for naming the new school. The controversy began when the board unanimously decided to name the school Thomas Jefferson High School. The debate over the name and the method for choosing it erupted immediately, leading to a petition to change the name to Crispus Attucks High School. This petition, which was eventually referred to the board's committee on instruction, was signed by Mrs. Robert Brokenburr, F. E. DeFrantz, secretary of the Senate Avenue YMCA, and a host of other community leaders.[28] Rev. E. H. White, pastor of Simpson ME Church, suggested the name Paul Lawrence Dunbar, while objecting to Crispus Attucks: "He was not a soldier, as a private citizen he simply rushed into the streets in front of the battle and lost his life."[29] Edgar Fitzpatrick, not caring for any of the names, dismissed Attucks, Jefferson, Dunbar, and Frederick Douglass in a carefully prepared letter. His idea was that some contemporary individual should be honored by having his or her name attached to this community monument.[30] After conferring with the "Colored P.T.A.," the board officially changed the name of the school from Jefferson to Crispus Attucks High School, and the protests seemed to subside, at least over this matter.[31]

After several inquiries from board members and interested citizens, board president Clemens Vonnegut announced that it was the adopted policy for all black high school pupils to attend Attucks upon its completion. There were no debates over this matter as the board seemed unified on this new policy.[32] In May Matthias Nolcox was appointed principal of Crispus Attucks High School at a salary of $3,800 per calendar year, as the first step toward staffing the newest Indianapolis public school.[33]

Gathering a faculty of quality on such short notice was no easy task, but Nolcox was up to the assignment. Locally, because

IHS C2250

Matthias Nolcox, Crispus Attucks High School principal, 1927–30

of limited higher education opportunities for blacks, hopes of assembling a qualified force of black teachers were not very bright; therefore, recruiting from distant places was the order of the day. The original faculty, as appointed by the board in 1927, underwent several changes prior to the opening of school, and even into the second year many additional faculty and staff appointments, both full and part-time, were made. One late appointment was the first white faculty member at Crispus Attucks High School, Sgt. Frank Whitlow, ROTC instructor.[34]

Although there had been strong protests against a separate high school, as the date for the opening of Crispus Attucks grew nearer excitement in the black community mounted. Many black teenagers who had withdrawn from other high schools for various reasons and others who had not entered high school with their original classes came to Crispus Attucks. This unanticipated enrollment made original plans for student body and staff obsolete before the first class was held. Original plans called for an enrollment of about 1,000 students, but that estimate soon rose to about 1,200. When the doors finally opened the total enrollment exceeded 1,350 students. In keeping with growing support from within the black community, the Women's Council, a local black organization, offered a one-hundred-dollar scholarship to the top student achiever each year, and a local merchants' association requested permission to have an open house, neighborhood decorations, and an opening day celebration at the school. These requests were approved by the board.[35] Not only was 1927 "the year of Crispus Attucks," but it also seemed to be a pivotal point in the separation-of-races issue. Prior to the school's opening, attorney W. S. Henry attempted to cut short the efforts of two or three blacks who were taking an "inside" poll among black workers at City Hospital to see if a separate unit for blacks was feasible.[36] The controversy served to heighten community interest in the pros and cons of separatism in general as the hospital issue continued to parallel school and housing problems for many years.

While school opened in September with the usual excitement, there were unusual events taking place. Approximately eighteen black students returned, with their parents, to Shortridge, Manual, and Tech high schools, expressing a desire to continue their previously planned courses of study. To complete

IHS C4257

Crispus Attucks High School

their academic studies the students needed courses in Spanish and trigonometry, which were not part of the originally announced curriculum at Attucks. The students were barred from these schools, and the superintendent refused to see several of them, a situation foreseen by those who had originally objected to a separate high school. The fact that there were several attorneys in this group fueled the fires of controversy, leading eventually to rumors of an impending test case.[37]

Circulation of this story around the state may well have helped trigger a student strike at Emerson High School in Gary, Indiana, about a week later. Twenty-four black students were transferred to Emerson to the dismay of white students and parents. White students left the school, continuing their protest with a parade through the downtown section of Gary. Signs reading "We won't go back until Emerson's white" were commonplace. Shortly thereafter, promises of a $15,000 temporary school for blacks, which was never built, and a $600,000 permanent facility, also for blacks, quieted the situation for the time being.[38] At what must have seemed like the same instant, trustees of Butler University in Indianapolis announced their decision to limit the number of black students entering the university to a maximum of ten each year. Strenuous objections to this move came immediately from the Interracial Committee of the Council of Social Agencies that appointed a special subcommittee to meet with the trustees.[39] From the eye of the storm, on 27 October 1927 the Crispus Attucks High School dedication ceremonies, designed by the school board to create an atmosphere in which it hoped black faculty and students would begin developing a sense of pride in the new school without dwelling on its long-term significance, proceeded as planned.

By mid-October 1927 the Gary situation was back in the headlines. William Pickens, NAACP field secretary, held a mass meeting in Gary of about three thousand people; more than $1,000 was raised to help in the fight against segregation. Attorney R. L. Bailey, chief counsel in the planned legal action, said, "The Indianapolis example, many Gary citizens feel, encouraged the whites of Gary, also a Klan center, to stage their local attempt."[40] The following week an injunction was granted, but it was only a matter of time before ground was broken for Gary Roosevelt High School, which was to be the "Crispus Attucks" of the northern part of the state. With the building of Evansville's Lincoln High School, located in the southernmost part of the state, the trilogy was completed by 1929. Those areas of the state with the largest black populations were prepared to offer segregated education in grades one through twelve. Refusing the admission of blacks to common schools established for the education of whites had been affirmed several times and was well on the way to being etched in stone.[41] It seemed obvious that the segregating of students in high school was only symptomatic of the desire of a large segment of the white population to create separate facilities in all walks of life; elementary schools and housing had led the way.

The northwestern part of Indianapolis, which included the home of the White People's Protective League's president, had become a rallying point for separatism. The organization sent circulars to real estate agents, rental agencies, and other parties announcing its territorial claims and decrying the movement of blacks into that part of the city. The threat to these agents was just as obvious as the threat to blacks seeking better housing. An interracial group from the Indianapolis Church Federation, recognizing the dangers inherent in this situation, issued a strong statement asking the police chief to stop distribution of the circulars.[42] The same newspapers that had lashed out at the Klan in 1924 allowed housing rental ads to carry color stipulations and showed no sign of protesting a new housing ordinance. Reaction to passage of the city council ordinance, with a Democratic councilman dissenting, left little doubt about the feeling of those present: "Loud cheering, hand-clapping and stamping of feet by more than 800 spectators marked the adoption by the City Council tonight of a race segregation ordinance which limits the districts in which colored persons may establish residence and forbids white persons residing in colored districts."[43] Prior to passage, the state attorney general and city corporate council had declared the move unconstitutional after investigating similar cases in Louisville and New Orleans. Since the ordinance did not restrict purchases, only the matter of where one could live was in question. Under the watchful eyes of the local and national NAACP, a friendly suit involving a housing transaction between Dr. Guy L. Grant, who was black, and Edward S. Gaillard was arranged. Grant reneged on his promise to purchase a house from Gaillard because its location was in a racially restrictive area, and he would not have been allowed to occupy the house under the new ordinance. In response to this case, Judge Harry O. Chamberlin of the Marion County Circuit Court ruled the housing segregation ordinance unconstitutional; it made the right of a legal resident of the state to live in or on his own property dependent on the consent of other citizens.[44]

The president of the White People's Protective League, undaunted by this temporary setback, sent a letter to famous Chicago attorney Clarence Darrow, which fanned the flames of prejudice. She scolded Darrow for his friendship with blacks and questioned what his reaction would be if one moved next door to him or married into his family. She even expressed the wish that he would marry one himself. In her closing lines she said, "SO, MR. NEGRO—Get busy hiking yourselves out of our white residential neighborhoods before you are notified to pay your fine assessment. . . . It will be a whole lot easier for these Negroes east of me to vacate now than it will be later on, for I am coming after them, I warn you!"[45] The following week a letter arrived inviting the league's president to speak before the Chicago Press Club. She declined saying that she "addresses white audiences only."[46]

In an attempt to keep blacks out of the "white community," only certain homes were shown to them, inflated prices were quoted, loans were not available for purchases in certain neighborhoods, and membership as "realtors" in the Indianapolis Real Estate Association was reserved for white citizens only.[47] The *Indianapolis News,* commenting on this series of events, printed the following as part of an editorial:

> One thing certainly should be done as soon as possible, and that is to pave the streets in colored neighborhoods, and make them so attractive that there will be no desire to get out of them. The colored people who move into white sections are not, as a rule, seeking to get away from their own people and into relations with the whites, but are moved by the desire to live in better surroundings. The surroundings should be made as good as those in white sections, so that there may be no reason for leaving them.[48]

Joseph C. Carroll, who later earned a Ph.D. from Ohio State University, was among those teachers hired in 1929, as the faculty of Crispus Attucks continued to grow. Carroll also was a distinguished national writer and an early advocate of teaching black history. It is very probable that Dr. Carroll introduced the study of black history to the Indianapolis public schools during his tenure at Crispus Attucks High School. With this notable exception, the Attucks curriculum was not very different from other high schools since standardization under regulations of the North Central Association was the norm by the late 1920s.[49]

To relieve overcrowding at Attucks, it was announced that School 17, located on the same city block, was to become part of the high school under jurisdiction of the Attucks principal.[50] Release of the 1930 school enumeration report confirmed a growing suspicion as it indicated a continued steady rise in the numbers of school-age blacks in Indianapolis; there were 37,033 white males and 36,035 white females as compared to 5,247 black males and 5,246 black females, an increase of more than fourfold in fifty years. The report dealt with ages six to twenty-one only.[51] Even though great interest in the elementary schools remained, particularly for those parents of children attending Public Schools 40, 42, and 87, attention of the black community continued to be focused on Crispus Attucks High School. It was one of a kind. In addition to providing good educational possibilities, the school served a true community center function following its initial baptism under fire.

In a letter from Henry Herod, secretary of the Interracial Committee of the Council of Social Agencies, a request was made to use the vacant area behind Attucks as a playground. At about the same time, the National Association of Colored Physicians expressed a desire to use the auditorium, cafeteria, and several rooms at Attucks for a convention the week of 18–22 August 1930. The requests were extraordinary, but both were approved unanimously by the school board.[52] This was doubtless an indication that the board was fully aware of the tenseness and underlying significance surrounding the "colored school situation."

In a surprising turn of events, the principalship of Crispus Attucks High School changed rather suddenly. In July 1930

Thomas J. Anderson from Pennsylvania replaced Matthias Nolcox, who was assigned to School 17 without public explanation. Anderson's tenure was short, ending about the time school opened in September. Reasons given for his departure were obscure, ranging from licensing difficulties to failure to get along with his staff. For his help in stabilizing a somewhat confused situation, Emory James, a teacher in the school, was awarded an extra stipend of one hundred dollars by the board for assisting with organizational duties during the month of August.[53] Naturally, the abrupt change was troublesome, but there was an air of expectation all around.

A principal was soon to be named signaling the beginning of what many hoped would be a new era at Crispus Attucks High School. Russell A. Lane, a member of the original faculty, was appointed as acting principal.[54] At the time, no one knew that he was to be principal of Attucks High School for many years and that the school would achieve national and even international fame because of its academic excellence, sports program, and its place in the civil rights arena. What antagonists did know was that finally local schools resembled Indianapolis society in general; they were now completely segregated and cradle-to-grave separation seemed within reach.

Notes

1. *Laws of Indiana,* 1869 (special sessions), 41. The bill experienced great difficulties because it was being considered at the same session as ratification of the Fourteenth Amendment to the United States Constitution. Many white southern immigrants to Indiana were less than fond of the principles in the proposed amendment, thereby putting them in no mood to give due consideration to a school bill for black student education.

2. Indianapolis Board of School Commissioners, Minutes, Book X, 63.

3. Ronald D. Cohen and Raymond A. Mohl, *The Paradox of Progressive Education: The Gary Plan and Urban Schooling* (Port Washington, N.Y.: Kennikat Press, 1979), 110–12.

4. Horace Mann Bond, *Education of the Negro in the American Social Order* (New York: Octagon Books, 1970), 199.

5. *Indianapolis News,* 11 June 1915. The article describes honors and activities of black Indianapolis students in the city high schools and previous graduates who were attending colleges.

6. *Indianapolis World,* 6 May 1921. The house at 2255 N. Capitol Avenue is currently located in a traditionally black community.

7. *The Fiery Cross,* 16 May 1924. Emma Lou Thornbrough's article, "Segregation in Indiana during the Klan Era of the 1920s," *Mississippi Valley Historical Review* 47 (Mar. 1961): 594–618, provides an excellent description of Klan activity in Indiana during the period 1920–30 along with good demographic information about selected cities in Indiana.

8. *The Fiery Cross,* 9 Feb. 1923.

9. Ibid., 2 May 1924.

10. Ibid., 8 Dec. 1922.

11. *Crisis* 29 (Jan. 1925): 131–32.

12. Minutes, Book X, 29–30 and 50–51. Other signatures on the letter of protest were Charles R. Durenbury, Mrs. Owen (Olive) Martin, Irven Armstrong, William F. Cannon, James I. Martin, B. S. Fisher, Estella Ballanger, Grace M. Hicks, Dr. Lucian B. Meriwether, Samuel A. Grizzle, Belle C. Norrell, Vera S. Gray, A. P. Kelly, and R. B. Smith.

13. Judy Jolley Mohraz, *The Separate Problem: Case Studies of Black Education in the North, 1900–1930* (Westport, Conn.: Greenwood Press, 1979).

14. Cohen and Mohl, *Paradox of Progressive Education,* 121.

15. Minutes, Book X, 63.

16. Minutes, Book W, 226.

17. Ibid., 226–27.

18. Ibid., 396–97. The Chamber of Commerce sent an earlier letter (June 1922) containing a similar request.

19. Minutes, Book X, 323. The $125,000 figure had been red-lined in the Board Minutes and $136,000 substituted.

20. Minutes, Book X, 235–36.

21. Ibid., 271.

22. Ibid., 286, 342; Thornbrough, "Segregation in Indiana during the Klan Era of the 1920s," 605; *Greathouse* v. *Board of School Commissioners of City of Indianapolis,* 198 Ind. 95–107 (1926–27); Lucas B. Willis to Moorfield Story, 1 June 1924, NAACP Papers, Legal File, Manuscript Division, Library of Congress.

23. Minutes, Book Z, 19.

24. Ibid., 473; Minutes, Book AA, 14.

25. F. B. Ransom to Walter F. White, 15 Jan. 1925, NAACP Legal File-Cases Supported, Jan.–Dec. 1925; W. S. Henry to Walter F. White, 18 Nov. 1924, ibid.; Walter F. White to Arthur B. Spingarn, 22 Nov. 1924, ibid., Manuscript Division, Library of Congress.

26. Minutes, Book Z, 19.

27. Minutes, Book AA, 47–48.

28. Ibid., 84 and Minutes, Book BB, 9. Other signers of the petition were Edward F. Gaillard, Dr. William Weir Stuart, Dr. M. D. Batties, May B. Belcher, J. H. Braxton, C. H. Watson, Arathor Edelen, Rev. S. B. Butler of Mt. Zion Church, F. A. Penn, M. DeArono McCarey, A. F. Moton, and Carl K. Wilbur.

29. Minutes, Book BB, 31.

30. Ibid., 61.

31. Ibid., 113.

32. Minutes, Book CC, 166.

33. Ibid., 251.

34. Indianapolis Public Schools, Teacher Directory, 1927–28, pp. 9, 32.

35. Minutes, Book BB, 412.

36. *Indianapolis Recorder,* 9 Apr. 1927.

37. Ibid., 24 Sept. 1927.

38. James B. Lane, *"City of the Century": A History of Gary, Indiana* (Bloomington: Indiana University Press, 1978), 141–47.

39. *Indianapolis Recorder,* 8 Oct. 1927. Members of the Council of Social Agencies were Rev. C. H. Winders, Dr. Alva W. Taylor, Rev. Henry C. Herod, Mary Belcher, Homer W. Borst, and Pearl B. Forsyth.

40. Ibid., 22 Oct. 1927.

41. *Greathouse* v. *Board of School Commissioners,* 95, 151, N.E. 411; *State, ex rel. Mitchell* v. *Gray et al., School Trustees,* 93 Ind. 303 (1883); *State, ex rel. Oliver et al.* v. *Grubb, Trustees,* 85 Ind. 213 (1882).

42. *Indianapolis Recorder,* 30 Jan. 1926.

43. *New York Times,* 17 Mar. 1926. There was one dissenting vote by Edward B. Raub. *Indianapolis News,* 16 Mar. 1926.

44. *Indianapolis News,* 16 Mar. 1926; *Crisis* 32 (May 1926): 24; *Indianapolis News,* 24 Nov. 1926.

45. *Indianapolis Recorder,* 24 July 1926.

46. Ibid., 31 July 1926.

47. *Indianapolis News,* 16 Mar. 1926.

48. Ibid., 24 Nov. 1926.

49. Minutes, Book FF, 185; *Indianapolis Recorder,* 10 Sept. 1927.

50. Minutes, Book FF, 121, 122. (School 17 was leveled in the summer of 1984. Historic preservationists wanted to save it because of its unique architecture and its landmark status as the earliest original black school in Indianapolis. The local school board voted to raze the building.)

51. Minutes, Book GG, 61.

52. Ibid., 75–80.

53. Ibid., 228.

54. Ibid., 249.

To All Classes; to All Races; This House Is Dedicated: The Walker Theatre Revisited

Gloria J. Gibson-Hudson

On Monday, 26 December 1927, the Walker Theatre opened its doors to the Indianapolis community. Freeman B. Ransom, attorney and general manager of the Walker Manufacturing Company, dedicated the building "to those who strive readily; to those who love good music, good pictures, high class entertainment . . . to all classes; to all races." Over sixty-five years have passed since that ceremony. Innumerable films have been screened, songs sung, steps danced, jokes told, and contests won. Down through the decades the watchful Egyptian sphinxes on either side of the stage have noted as one artistic period merged into another.

As the years went by, the glorious splendor of a beautiful theater gave way to decay. From available evidence, it appears that the doors closed for the last time in the late 1970s. The African motifs would hibernate for many years; in fact, they would lay dormant until Friday, 14 October 1988. As this article projects images of the old Walker Theatre, some theatergoers can reminisce about the enjoyable hours spent there. Others

Madam C. J. Walker Collection, IHS C2139

Sarah Breedlove Walker founded the Walker Manufacturing Company and relocated her business from Denver to Indianapolis in 1910.

can begin to learn of the theater's genesis, peaks of activity, demise, and subsequent rebirth.

According to historical accounts, Madam C. J. Walker was visiting the office of her manufacturing company in Indianapolis. After her meeting, she and a friend simply wanted "to go to the movies." However, when she tried to purchase a ticket, she was discouraged from doing so. Since the early days of slavery, black people had heard the dissonant resonance of these words. Phrases such as "no colored," "whites only," and "colored use back door" were among those branded into the visual and men-

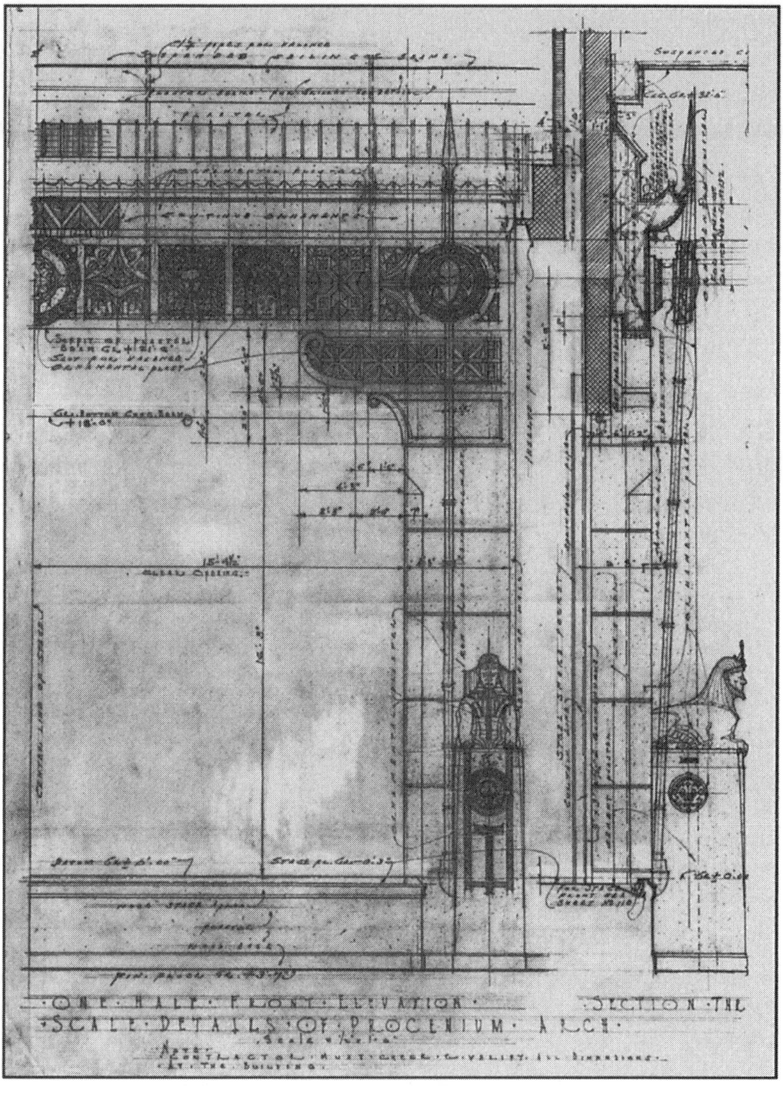

IHS C4091

Original architectural drawings for the Walker Theatre building, designed by Rubush and Hunter tal psyche of black Americans. For many, the only response was no response at all. Quiet acceptance amidst internal anger and turmoil became the status quo.

For Madam Walker the raging societal volcano spewing ash of racial injustice had to be confronted. Quiet acceptance was not the answer. The only solution was a direct assault. First, she decided to file suit against the Central Amusement Company, which operated the Isis Theatre located at 113 North Illinois Street. The suit, filed in 1915, alleged that the theater attendant attempted to charge Walker a greater than usual price because of her race, and she refused to pay. Secondly, she envisioned a theater building for her people: a facility where blacks could momentarily forget about racial barriers and enjoy themselves. Unfortunately, Madam Walker died in 1919 before her plans could materialize.

A few years later, Madam Walker's daughter, A'Lelia Walker, decided that she would construct a building in honor of her mother. Working in collaboration with F. B. Ransom, they contemplated a structure that would serve not only as an artistic haven, but also as a facility offering services for all those affected by racism. The Walker Theatre building was "built to serve as the social and cultural center of Indianapolis."[1]

The Walker Manufacturing Company purchased the land in 1924 for $58,000. Receipts indicate a mortgage loan was taken out in 1924 from the Fletcher-American Company and repaid in full three years later. The minutes of the 5 January 1928 board meeting explained the relationship between the manufacturing company and the theater company.

> That the Mme. C. J. Walker Manufacturing Company enter into a verbal agreement with the Walker Theatre Company, said Walker Theatre Company to operate the Walker Theatre with the understanding that the Walker Theatre Company pay the Mme. C. J. Walker Mfg. Company an annual rental in the sum of fifteen thousand ($15,000) a year, with the further understanding that such rental be divided

Bass Photo Collections IHS C2142

The Walker Theatre building was erected in 1927.

> in twelve equal monthly payments and that the same shall be paid monthly in advance.

In addition to the theater, the building housed the Walker Casino, the Walker Beauty Shop, the Walker Drug Store, the Walker Coffee Pot, and numerous offices.

The theater, however, was the most lavish part of the structure. Designed by the white architectural firm of Rubush and Hunter, the overall theme reflected motifs of African culture. The spears, monkeys, striking sphinxes, and Moorish-style arches enabled black visitors to take pride in their heritage.

The theater would book only the "highest quality" entertainment as upward mobility was very important in the late 1920s.

Madam C. J. Walker Collection, IHS A77

Freeman B. Ransom

The opening ceremony, on Monday, 26 December 1927, included the film *The Magic Flame,* starring Ronald Coleman and Vilma Banky. Reginald DuValle's band, "The Blackbirds," provided the music along with Mary Singleton at the "golden-voiced Barton pipe-organ." The *Indianapolis News* reported on 27 December 1927, "Two changes of feature films a week, organ selections and short reels is the present policy of the house." F. B. Ransom served as general manager, and Charles Erwin was house manager.

Ticket prices ranged from fifteen to forty cents. Opening night box office receipts indicate there was a packed house, and the theater grossed over a thousand dollars. Walker Theatre records dating from 1927 to 1930, located at the Indiana

Historical Society Library (M399), reveal film titles, musical performers, attendance, money received, and even weather conditions. During the early years the black-owned and operated theater appeared financially sound while ironically the economic conditions that surrounded it were in ruins. So severe was the devastation that A'Lelia Walker would later be forced to close her beloved Dark Towers night spot in New York. The theater, however, survived.

In a recent interview attorney Willard Ransom, son of F. B. Ransom, explained that during the early years the Walker Theatre flourished because of segregation and community cohesion, and because black people needed an oasis for escape. Films, jazz, and vaudeville provided that oasis amidst the oppression and degradation of everyday life during the depression.

From the very beginning films were an integral component of the Walker Theatre entertainment and contributed immensely to its financial prosperity. *The Magic Flame* was a white film, billed as a "smashing success." It had been shown in metropolitan areas, and now blacks in Indianapolis had an opportunity to view it in a luxurious setting, and not in the "colored balcony." During the late twenties and early thirties the Walker Theatre continued to book white mainstream Hollywood films. Available evidence does not point to screening of films by early black filmmakers such as Oscar Micheaux or the Lincoln Motion Picture Company (George P. and Noble Johnson). Black companies did not have funds for mass production or national advertising and distribution. Consequently, films such as Micheaux's *The House behind the Cedars* (1927) or *The Scar of Shame* (1928) by the Colored Players Company and other black films appear not to have been shown there.

The "coloring" of vaudeville was a different story. Starting in March 1928 the Walker Theatre presented "hot sizzling acts." The premiere act under the "new and better policy" was Rector and Cooper. Eddie Rector, who had performed in Harlem, was billed as the "smoothest sand dancer of all." Ralph Cooper was considered a rising celebrity. He would later become an official in the Million Dollar Film Company and share star billing with Lena Horne in the film *The Duke Is Tops* (1938). The review in the *Indianapolis Recorder,* 17 March 1928, stated, "The orchestra is directed by Eddie, while Ralph introduces the other features and directs the chorus, oh boy! Costumed out of this world and can they dance." A'Lelia Walker was in attendance for this show in March 1928. Admission was thirty-five cents.

On the surface it seemed as if the films and vaudeville acts were running smoothly. Behind the scenes, the theater was failing financially. The minutes of the 12 January 1930 board meeting state:

> F. B. Ransom, general manager, reported failure in the part of the Walker Theatre Company to pay rent and that the Walker Theatre Company was indebted to the Mme. C. J. Walker Mfg. Company, for back rent, and it appears from the statement of the Walker Theatre Company, said Company is not only unable to pay anything on the back rent, but cannot pay on the current rent, after due discussion it was agreed that the Walker Theatre Company be permitted to operate the Walker Theatre only until the Walker Mfg. Company is able to find a tenant for said theatre.

Attorney Willard Ransom stated that the Walker Theatre Company ran the facility only during part of the 1930s. The first outside manager he remembered was white businessman Dudley Williston, who continued to book films and shows of interest to the black community. During the 1930s the theater showcased talent from the Theatre Owners Booking Association (TOBA), or "Tough on Black Asses," as blacks sometimes referred to it. The TOBA was the black answer to the vaudeville circuit. The Whitman Sisters were a part of the circuit, as were Butterbeans and Susie, who appeared at the Walker in the 1930s.

Mainstream white Hollywood films such as *The Mighty,* starring George Bancroft and Ester Ralston, continued to be programmed at the theater. In addition, Indianapolis was treated to several bookings of Ethel Waters. Admission was now fifty cents.

The 1939 Academy Awards aroused unusual interest and excitement among blacks from coast to coast. That year Hattie McDaniel made history; she was the first black actress to be nominated for, and to receive, an Oscar. The *Indianapolis Recorder* ran a long feature article on McDaniel and her supporting role in the classic *Gone with the Wind.* After she won the award, many thought this was a clear indication that blacks would receive increased roles in Hollywood. Moreover, they felt the climate of race relations would improve for all black Americans. In retrospect, racism did not die, nor did its exclusionary force diminish during this period.

A few years later Hollywood produced two segregated musicals, *Cabin in the Sky* and *Stormy Weather.* These films had all-star casts, including Lena Horne, Ethel Waters, Eddie Anderson, and Bill Robinson. Although both were entertaining, they had no apparent social or cultural relevance. Furthermore, in no way did they advance the "Double V" wartime goal—victory abroad against fascism and victory at home against racism.

The 1950s and 1960s brought more Hollywood films to the Walker Theatre, including those starring Sidney Poitier. He was well received by both blacks and whites. In his early films blacks liked him because he was a "clean-cut" hero; whites liked him because he was safe—racially "non-threatening."

The theater closed for a while in the early 1960s but reopened in December 1965. Headlines on the *Recorder* social page read, "All Star Revue, Go-Go Girls Set for Gala Walker Theatre." Ralph Trotter served as operator of the theater. In an appeal in the 27 November 1965 *Recorder,* Trotter promised the citizens of Indianapolis that he would try at all times to give them lively entertainment and at the same time guarantee good order in the theater. The article noted that performers would change from time to time but that the popular Go-Go Girls would remain constant. Finally, he informed black theatergoers that the Walker and the *Recorder* would resume a holiday tradition: they would host the eighteenth annual Christmas Midnite Benefit Show on 18 December from midnight until 3:30 A.M.

During the late 1960s and into the mid-1970s the theater once again flourished with activity. The "blacksploitation" era was in full swing. These films, many released by white Hollywood studios, were produced at a phenomenal pace. Pam Grier, for example, starred in over a dozen films within approximately five years. Blacks in Indianapolis and other metropolitan areas flocked to the theaters to see films such as *Super Fly, The Mack,* and *Foxy Brown.*

The Walker Theatre booked many "blacksploitation" films, including *Kung Fu Mama, Tricky Baby, Black Sampson,* and Bruce Lee's *The Young Dragon.* Many of these films contained no real plot. The one dimensional central characters included drug pushers, prostitutes, pimps, murderers, and a crooked white-power establishment. Black women were portrayed in almost every conceivable negative stereotype. Writing on the history of black and Hispanic women in film, Elizabeth Hadley Freydberg notes, "The women in these films [blacksploitation] were incidental; they created the 'ambiance' of the ghetto as prostitutes, whores, and drug addicts."[2] Specifically, Freydberg points out:

> In *Foxy Brown* (1974) alone, [Pam] Grier beats up a call girl in a bar, slashes the throat of another woman, burns two men to death, castrates a third and delivers the genitals in a pickle jar to the leader of a vice ring as a warning.[3]

By the late 1970s blacks grew tired of these films, realizing that they generally provided only negative role models for black youth. Consequently, the blacksploitation genre died as quickly as it had emerged. Innumerable black actors and actresses had received widespread exposure and substantial incomes. Paradoxically, for many stars, as the blacksploitation era came to a close, so too did their careers in Hollywood.

The last person to lease the theater was Walter Eagleson in 1978. Because the theater was deteriorating and in the process of being sold, Eagleson did not run the theater for the entire three-year period of his lease. Although an exact date for the closing is not known, it is believed the doors finally closed in late 1978 or early 1979.

For approximately fifty years the theater provided black Indianapolis residents with major films and live performances, featuring prominent dancers, singers, comedians, jazz musicians, and local amateur talent shows. Black residents had rendered substantial support for theater activities throughout its history. When the Walker Theatre opened in 1927 it was part of the limited entertainment options available for blacks in segregated Indianapolis. When the theater closed a half century later, a desegregating city was hard at work ushering in a new social order. In the interim, blacks had marched, sang, protested, and died for equal rights. Blacks would no longer have to hear the echo of the words Madam Walker endured, "for whites only."

Almost ten years after the theater's doors closed, they were opened once again. Today, the theater is a part of the Madame Walker Urban Life Center, with Josephine Weathers as the executive director. As part of the theater's reopening activities, the Black Film Center/Archive (Department of Afro-American Studies, Indiana University) and the Walker staff, with the assistance of other Indianapolis arts agencies, brought film back to Indiana Avenue. A week-long conference entitled "Freedom: A Lens on Black America and the Third World," screened works by contemporary filmmakers who addressed various aspects of liberation. The films chosen for the festival served as indicators of, and perceptions about, black life in America and South Africa.

The festival opened on Saturday, 15 October 1988, with a dialogue between award-winning novelist Alex Haley and

A'Lelia Bundles, great-great-granddaughter of Madam C. J. Walker. The discussion concerned their research on a novel Haley was writing on Walker. The evening provided a rare opportunity not only to learn more about the experiences of Madam Walker, but also allowed audiences to gain insight into how thoughts and experiences are translated into both literary and, subsequently, cinematic form.

Sunday was billed as a family matinee. Sidney Poitier returned to the Walker screen in a much different role. In *Buck and the Preacher* he portrayed a cowboy and ex-cavalryman, leading blacks westward after the Civil War. Although fictional, the film educated audiences to the plight and contributions of blacks settling the West.

On Monday night, filmmaker Stanley Nelson was invited to share his insights and experiences with aspiring black filmmakers throughout the state. Nelson's film, *Two Dollars and a Dream,* was also screened. An enthusiastic audience asked Nelson many personal, in-depth questions about filmmaking.

Two films entitled *Mandela* were presented the following evening. A documentary was shown in its entirety, and excerpts from an HBO feature film were screened. Both works focused on the life of Winnie Mandela and the struggle against apartheid. Patrick O'Meara, director of the African Studies Program at Indiana University, presented authoritative introductory remarks to alert the audience to the differences in the two films. Following the screening, the audience directed questions to documentary filmmaker Peter Davis and Seboko Monamodi, a black South African student at Indiana University.

On Wednesday, filmmaker William Miles presented his documentary, *Men of Bronze.* The film examines the contributions of blacks to the military during the First World War. Archival film and rare photographs are interwoven with interviews from the highly decorated 369th Infantry Regiment. In addition, Miles shared clips from his current film project on author James

Baldwin. He hoped to complete the ninety-minute documentary in 1989 and promised an Indianapolis premiere.

Filmmaker Julie Dash discussed her unique perspective regarding the struggle for artistic freedom facing black women artists. Two of her works, *Four Women* and *Illusions,* were shown. *Four Women* uses a song text to communicate the cultural history of black Americans. It is a dance film utilizing stylized movements and attire to express the metamorphosis of black women from Africa to their struggle for survival in America. The film is a visualization of the famous ballad written and performed by Nina Simone. *Illusions* explores the fine line between illusion and reality that sometimes occurs in life. Set during World War II, the film dramatizes various levels of illusion, including those centered around racial identity, status, and the film industry. Dash also brought clips from her current film project, *Daughters of the Dust.* When completed, she will be the first black woman to produce a 35mm film.

The film festival closed with a Hollywood production, *Cry Freedom,* starring Denzel Washington as Steven Biko. Professor C. R. D. Halisi, a political scientist, provided insight into apartheid and discussed his experiences in South Africa and his relationship with Biko. He also commented on what the film accomplishes and what it does not. His commentary stimulated a lively discussion and elicited many probing questions. After a lengthy interchange the evening ended. More than a thousand Indiana residents attended the week-long festival events.

The Walker Theatre renaissance represents more than the mere reopening of a place of entertainment. It is a vital component of Indiana's cultural history dating back to 1927. Throughout the years, the black community has always supported the theater. The present staff strives to revive the tradition of excellence established by Madam C. J. Walker and thereby help restore "the Avenue" to its former brilliance. The theater's renaissance promises to provide its supporters with exciting, provocative, insightful, and culturally meaningful entertainment as Indianapolis moves into the twenty-first century.

NOTES

1. Patricia J. Casler, "The Architecture of Rubush and Hunter" (Master's thesis, Columbia University, 1985), 91.

2. Elizabeth Hadley Freydberg, "Prostitutes, Concubines, Whores, and Bitches: Black and Hispanic Women in Contemporary American Film," in *Women of Color: Perspectives on Feminism and Identity,* ed. Audrey T. McCluskey, Women's Study Program, vol. 1, no. 1 (Bloomington: Indiana University, 1985), 55.

3. Ibid., 55, 56.

Women

The History of Black Women in Indiana

Emma Lou Thornbrough

Until recently, black Americans were largely ignored by historians or were only briefly mentioned in history books. When they were mentioned, they tended to be portrayed as stereotypes or even treated as a passive force. This has changed dramatically. In the last two decades some of the best research and writing in American history has dealt with the part that blacks have played in the shaping of history, and this research has caused us to gain new perspectives and to look at all of American history in new ways. But most of the research in black history has been about black men. Only very recently have historians begun to discover that black women, too, have a history.

Perhaps the most striking thing about the writing of the history of all women until very recently was simply that women were seldom mentioned. And when occasionally they did make it into the pages of a book, it was as the mother, wife, or mistress of a famous man and not in their own right. The role of women in history has been traditionally regarded as passive and supportive.

There is also anonymity about women that offers some difficulties in doing research about them. It is difficult to identify them because they were not considered worth mentioning, and often records about them were not preserved. Until very recently, there were few collections of women's papers in the manuscript collections of great libraries.

Traditionally, women were not supposed to be creative, therefore they had little opportunity to gain recognition in the arts. But women as mothers and as the gentler and weaker sex were expected to be the preservers and transmitters of culture.

All these generalities, which applied to the history of all women, were compounded in the case of black women. It certainly was not true that black women were not capable of being artistically creative.

Of course, what we know about the past depends upon the evidence that survives—usually literary, written evidence, although historians are learning to use other kinds of evidence. Nevertheless, much of the past is irrevocably lost, and this is more true of the history of blacks and women than of most fields of history because they often did not write letters, keep diaries, or make speeches; and when they did, these were seldom considered worth preserving. Women were seldom mentioned in newspapers. Those who were mentioned usually were "leaders" or at least were members of the upper or middle classes, which means that history is slanted toward these groups.

One of the most obvious differences between the life-styles of white women and black women, until very recently, has been in employment outside the home. Traditionally, white women might be gainfully employed for a few years before marriage, but once they were married, the vast majority became housewives, and it was unusual for a married woman to have a job or career outside the home. Economic necessity compelled most black women, married or unmarried, with or without children, to earn money by outside employment.

Because of the lack of education and discriminatory hiring practices throughout history, most black women have been compelled to work in the most menial, poorest paying jobs. All kinds of employment and income studies show that, on average, white males command the highest pay; black men are next on the scale; then white women; while black women are the lowest paid of any group. In Indiana, decade after decade, United States census reports show that the vast majority of black women have been in unskilled jobs—working in domestic service as waitresses, laundresses, and charwomen. Only since the Second World War have sizable numbers of black women found employment in industry, and only more recently in white-collar jobs. Of course, a few black women with requisite training found positions as teachers, but others with college degrees sometimes worked in menial jobs.

There are always exceptions, and a few black women became successful entrepreneurs, usually on a small scale, or succeeded in other nontraditional occupations. The most notable success story—Madam C. J. Walker. She was born in Louisiana, just after the Civil War, the child of ex-slave parents. She was married, a mother, and a widow while still in her teens. After the death of her husband, she and her daughter moved to St. Louis, where she worked as a laundress. She developed her own hairdressing and cosmetic formulas. After establishing headquarters in Indianapolis, her business grew into an international enterprise. The company maintained schools throughout the United States. Madam Walker sought to have the young women who were enrolled in these schools trained not only in beauty culture but also prepared to become useful, socially aware members of the community. Throughout her career, Madam Walker was noted as much as a philanthropist as a businesswoman. Examples of her gifts and charities are too numerous to mention in detail, but among them were scholarships for Tuskegee Institute and support for many programs which aided the poor.

In black society—in which most women worked outside the home for long hours, often at menial, physically exhausting drudgery—time for social and community activities was obviously limited. In the black community, as in the white, most of the leadership for women's activities came from educated, middle-class women who had some leisure, but in the black community a surprisingly large number of women from the humblest occupations managed to participate in church and community activities.

There were parallels and similarities between the organizations and activities of black women and white women, but for the most part the black and white communities were separate worlds. There were few shared experiences.

Most historians agree that the most influential institution in the black community has been the church. During slavery and since, religious faith has enabled blacks to survive and endure psychologically. The church has also been a center for social and charitable activities, has promoted education, and has helped develop black leaders. For black women, even more than for black men, perhaps, the church offered not only a source of psychological strength, but also opportunities for self-fulfillment and service because women were barred from other fields of activity open to men.

Of course, in black churches, as in white congregations, women were expected to serve God and church in modest, self-effacing ways. A good example of the typical male point of view was expressed in a little book on the history of the Second Baptist Church, one of the oldest black churches in Indianapolis. Moses Broyles, the minister who was one of the most important leaders in the black community during the Civil War and afterwards, wrote the book. In the book in which he discusses his own marriage, Broyles advised ministers to marry "a steady, high-toned Christian wife, who is affectionate to him and to the members, [who] strengthens the influence of a pastor among the members." He added:

> When they live together in harmony, as they should and conduct their family in order, they set an example to the membership generally. Ministers should therefore select the most pious, steady, and economical women for their wives, and endeavor to live in harmony with them.

Although women might be valued as ministers' wives to furnish examples of piety and fidelity to the congregation, other aspirations of the weaker sex were frowned upon by black preachers. There were a few examples of black women evangelists, and the appearance of one of them in Indianapolis in 1904 evidently caused consternation among the male preachers. In a letter which sounds surprisingly modern in tone, a few courageous women came to her defense and flayed the ministers for their effort to silence her. "It is indeed singular what unwarranted excitement and uneasiness has suddenly seized upon a few of our colored Baptist pastors since the recent appearance in this city of a most wonderful, captivating, highly esteemed colored female preacher," they wrote in a letter to the press. They added:

> The day for nourishing all women on the doctrine that they are simply to look to the food, raiment and shelter of the male preacher, and then are "out of their places" to enter the very rostrums their sex has labored most to build to preach the same gospel that our brethren preach, we repeat . . . that day is a thing of the past. . . . For the preachers of the male sex to attempt to build an impassable hedge about themselves by rudely censuring and crushing by mere external force, those of our own sex is a sad mistake and the only real evil consequent upon female preachers of whatever denomination.

As this letter suggests, women traditionally played important parts in raising money to support the church and pay the pastor.

They also served the church in many other ways—through missionary societies, Sunday schools, the church choirs, and church-related charitable activities. In communities where many members were poverty-stricken and often were recent migrants from the rural South who needed assistance in adjusting to a new and sometimes hostile environment, black churches performed important welfare and charitable functions.

For example, in Terre Haute in 1914 members of the aid societies of the black churches cooperated in setting up a day nursery in a neighborhood where many women worked to support their families and who were often forced to leave their babies in the care of small children. The nursery was established, even though the church members supporting it had scarcely enough money to sustain their own families. The matron of the nursery worked without wages and took in washings in order to support herself.

Many of the women's clubs had religious ties and met in churches. In the black community it is often difficult to draw a line between the religious and the secular.

In all these activities, women showed initiative, resourcefulness, and organizational ability, but in the eyes of society their role was primarily one of moral uplift. One example was an address given by a man to the Sisters of Charity, one of the most important of the church-related women's organizations. As reported in the press, the speaker "took the occasion to remind the good sisters and ladies generally that they held the keys of the door through which all men must pass in order to reach the high standards of morality necessary to make good citizens; and they should exert themselves to make their influence felt throughout the community in this direction."

The words of the speaker on the influence of women were more clearly related to the role of teachers than women church workers. Certainly one of the most significant contributions of black women has been in education. Among a population where oftentimes the entire family had to work in order to exist, keeping children in school meant sacrifices. Sometimes daughters received more schooling because they were not compelled to go to work at such an early age as their brothers. This probably was one of the reasons why there was a relatively large group of educated women. For example, the first black to graduate from Indianapolis High School (later Shortridge High School) was a girl who graduated in 1876. The first black to graduate from Butler College was Gertrude Mahorney, who graduated in 1887 and later achieved notable success as a teacher in the Indianapolis schools—the only black teacher in the system who taught German.

Only a modest number of blacks graduated from high school before the First World War and only a small handful from colleges and universities until after World War II. Most of the young women attended teacher training schools. Several attended the Blaker Teachers College in Indianapolis. It opened in 1882.

Teaching in the segregated public schools was virtually the only vocation open to educated blacks, particularly women. Consequently, teachers enjoyed more prestige and furnished more leadership in the black community far more than they did in the white community. Black women teachers exerted incalculable influence in the classroom as well as in civic and cultural life.

In her book, *When the Truth Is Told,* Darlene Clark Hine outlined the remarkable career of Sallie Wyatt Stewart, a member of a poverty-stricken family, who worked her way through high school and teacher training institutions and taught for fifty years in the black schools of Evansville, teaching every grade from the first through high school. As a teacher, she introduced new courses of study, including domestic science. She was also a successful businesswoman. She and her husband amassed an estate of more than $100,000, much of which she left for the purpose of helping young black girls. Largely through her efforts, a day nursery for black children and the Evansville branch of the Phyllis Wheatley Young Women's Christian Association were founded, and the scholarship fund of the Indiana State Federation of Colored Women's Clubs was established.

In Indianapolis, one of the notable black teachers was Mary Cable, who received her early education in Kansas and later studied at Indiana University, the University of Chicago, and Columbia University. She worked in the Indianapolis public schools for forty years as teacher, principal, and director of student teaching. As a teacher, she sought to compensate for the culturally limited background of her pupils, many of whom were migrants from the South, and emphasized academic subjects and good citizenship. She was also very active in civic affairs.

The influence of teachers extended far beyond the schools. Women teachers were leaders in the club movement and in other organizations that are as much a significant part of the black community today as they have been since the beginning of free black communities in the United States.

Free blacks founded mutual aid societies and other kinds of private organizations as early as the era of the American Revolution. They were a manifestation of efforts at self-help and sharing which have always been characteristics of black society. There has been a black Masonic order since the days of the Revolutionary War. After the Civil War, secret fraternal organizations proliferated. There have always been women's auxiliaries to these male lodges, but women also formed a great many other kinds of clubs and societies. Some of them were purely social, but not many. Nearly all of them had other objectives as well: social and cultural uplift and service to the less fortunate.

As the number of educated women grew, they furnished the impetus and leadership for many clubs. Certainly part of the motivation was the W. E. B. Du Bois concept of the "Talented Tenth," the small, educated minority who would furnish the leadership for uplifting the masses.

The number of women's clubs was enormous. One organizing pioneer and an extraordinary person was Lillian Thomas Fox, a journalist in a period when there were few women in that profession. She was the first black reporter on the *Indianapolis News*, where she was employed for several years. She also had a reputation as a public speaker. In 1903 she brought together a group of women, many of them teachers (a rather elite gathering) in her home, where they agreed to form the Woman's Improvement Club. The name itself suggests the ideals and purposes: self-improvement for the members themselves and also community improvement. The group was typical of many women's clubs in devoting some of the programs to literature. It began by studying some examples of literature by or about black writers—the poetry of Phillis Wheatley, the life of Sojourner Truth, and the recently published volume by W. E. B. Du Bois, *The Souls of Black Folk*. Later, the club sponsored lectures by well-known blacks, including Mary Church Terrell and Du Bois. In the realm of community service the club sought to combat tuberculosis, a disease which took a fearful toll among blacks. For years the club raised funds to support a fresh-air camp.

Many other women's groups concerned themselves with support of efforts to improve medical and health services. In Indianapolis the only hospital that admitted blacks was City Hospital, and then only in one segregated ward with only a few available beds. Black physicians were barred, and there were no provisions for black interns or the training of black nurses. Other hospitals in the city accepted no black patients whatsoever. Similar conditions prevailed throughout the state.

In efforts to remedy the situation, blacks tried to maintain their own private hospitals, staffed with black physicians and nurses. These institutions were inadequate to meet the needs of the black population, but they represented an admirable effort at self-help. One of the activities of women's clubs was to raise funds for these hospitals.

The Sisters of Charity, founded in 1874 for the purpose of providing health care for the poor, expanded into a network of women's lodges throughout the state and succeeded in opening a small hospital that survived for a few years in the era of the

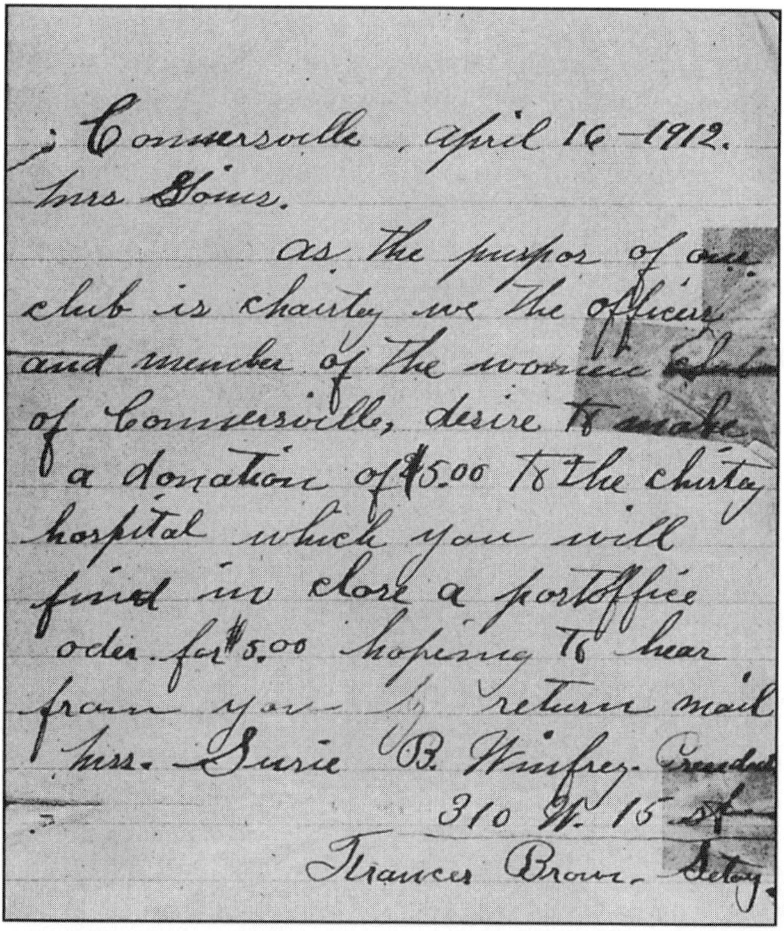

Connersville, April 16-1912.
Mrs Jones.
As the purpos of our club is charity we the officers and member of the women club of Connersville, desire to make a donation of $5.00 to the charity hospital which you will find in close a postoffice order for $5.00 hoping to hear from you by return mail
Mrs. Susie B. Winfrey - President
310 W. 15 St
Frances Brown - Sectry.

IHS C4421

Several Sisters of Charity lodges and various women's clubs in Indiana supported the Sisters of Charity State Hospital in Indianapolis.

First World War. About the same time, Lincoln Hospital, which received some public funding, was in operation in Indianapolis. Black women organized auxiliaries that sponsored fairs and other fund-raising activities for the hospital.

Another enterprise was the Alpha Home for the Aged founded in 1883 in Indianapolis. Elizabeth Goff, a former slave who worked as a maid for an Indianapolis family, conceived the idea for the home. She was concerned about the plight of aged black women servants like herself who had no relatives to care for them. As a beginning, her employer, Pauline Merritt, donated a small house. The governing board of the home was made up of women. The first residents were all women and all former slaves. Later, elderly men who were former slaves were also admitted. Under the guidance of the women board members and with the support of women's clubs, funds were raised which enabled the home to be moved to larger quarters. In 1914 the Alpha Home received a substantial endowment from Madam Walker.

In 1904, at the initiative of Lillian Thomas Fox, the Indiana State Federation of Colored Women's Clubs was organized. The National Association of Colored Women, with which the Indiana group was affiliated, had formed ten years earlier. It was similar in organization to the General Federation of Women's Clubs, the white women's group, but was separate from it. In that period most white women were either indifferent to or unaware of black women's groups or were actively opposed to association with them. A notable exception was May Wright Sewall, one of the most important women in the history of Indianapolis and a figure of national and international importance. She was one of the founders of the Indianapolis Museum of Art as well as the founder of the Propylaeum and the school that became Tudor Hall. Sewall also was one of the leading feminists of her generation and the founder of the National Council of Women and the International Council of Women. Unlike most of her contemporaries, May Wright Sewall was actively interested in black women and their problems. It is an interesting coincidence that she was the principal speaker at the organizational meeting of the Indiana State Federation of Colored Women's Clubs. In Indiana, as in other states, the state federation included clubs from all over the state. All clubs working on "religious, moral, educational, or charitable lines" were invited to affiliate. The first meeting adopted a preamble that indicated the philosophy and purpose

Courtesy of Suzanne Rollins

Indiana State Federation of Colored Women's Clubs Home, Indianapolis

of the women: "We, the colored women of the state of Indiana, feeling the need of organized effort, and intending to furnish evidence of material, mental and moral progress made by our people, do hereby unite in a state federation."

The officers of the state federation included the most able and influential women in the state. Certainly one of the most notable was Sallie Wyatt Stewart of Evansville, mentioned earlier. She was president of the federation from 1921 to 1928. Under her leadership, a scholarship fund was established, the federation focused more attention on social problems, and the membership was greatly expanded. In 1928 Stewart was elected president of the National Association of Colored Women. In 1930 she went to Vienna, Austria, as a delegate to the meeting of the International Council of Women.

Although most of the attention of women's organizations was directed toward improving the condition of blacks through self-help programs, from the very beginning they also gave some attention to public issues and public policies that affected the race. For example, at the first state convention of the Indiana State Federation of Colored Women's Clubs resolutions were adopted that deplored the spread of lynching and the increase in disfranchisement in the South.

By the time of the First World War, educated black women were beginning to put less emphasis on the self-help approach of Booker T. Washington as a solution to race problems. W. E. B. Du Bois was emerging as a significant influence on black intellectuals, and Indiana women were beginning to turn their attention to political and civil rights. These were the years when the long fight for the right of women to vote was drawing to an end. The Nineteenth Amendment to the United States Constitution was adopted just after the First World War.

The average black woman, like many white women, was not likely to be much interested in politics or the right to vote. For most black women politics probably seemed irrelevant to their central concern, especially if they looked at the political powerlessness of black men. But educated black women, like educated white women, sought the vote. Suffrage clubs, affiliated with the white women's groups, generally made up of black women but also including some men, were formed. At the meetings, public policies and the need for political action were discussed. There was increasing protest over the failure of government to recognize and protect the rights of black citizens.

In Anderson, for example, a Colored Civic Club was organized in 1915. At the first meeting, a young woman presented a report outlining some grievances among Anderson blacks—the condition of the schools, the denial of the use of public parks and tennis courts to blacks—all of them maintained by taxpayers' money. Why, the young women asked, did not blacks, as taxpayers, have the rights guaranteed to them by law? Just three years before the Anderson meeting, a group had been organized in Indianapolis to address the questions asked in

Bass Photo Collection, IHS C3411

The Phyllis Wheatley Young Women's Christian Association in Indianapolis provided young African-American tennis enthusiasts an opportunity for recreational enjoyment, ca. 1927.

Anderson—why black citizens were denied the rights guaranteed to them by law.

Closely related to the beginnings of women's interest in attaining the vote was growing interest in civil rights—constitutional and legal rights. From the beginning, women have played a significant part in the struggle for civil rights. In Indiana they began to work in an organized fashion when they formed the Indianapolis branch of the National Association for the Advancement of Colored People (NAACP) in 1912. The NAACP was first organized in 1909. It originated with a group made up primarily of white New York citizens (lawyers, philanthropists, and social workers) who were appalled at the deteriorating racial conditions in the United States, especially the growth of racial violence in the early years of the twentieth century. A few distinguished blacks like Du Bois and Ida Wells-Barnett were among the founders of the national association, and blacks have always predominated the local branches. The purpose of the organization was to fight such things as lynching, denial of voting rights, and Jim Crow laws and practices, primarily through litigation in the courts and lobbying.

In Indianapolis Mary Cable and the Colored Women's Civic Club, of which she was president, took the initiative. The Indianapolis branch was chartered in 1912, which made it the second oldest branch in the Midwest. Cable was the first president, and all the other officers and members of the first executive board were also women, a fact that made the Indianapolis branch unique.

A report that Cable wrote to the national office about the first year of the Indianapolis group states the reasons that motivated the women. The spirit of service and the desire to help the less fortunate, which characterized church groups and women's clubs, were evident, but there was also a new note of militancy in the demands for the end of discrimination and recognition of citizenship rights. The report told of efforts to enroll members: "We have done much to convince the indifferent that a membership fee would aid much in helping the downtrodden brother who has fewer privileges." But she expressed discouragement over the failure of many members of the black community to unite to fight discrimination. "We have suffered from discrimination," she said. But "we have not been sufficiently aroused to forget trivial differences that exist and so we are in small groups struggling against a division of opinion as to whether to continue waiting passively or to demand our rights." She feared that: "It will take a torrent that will almost sweep us from our feet before we will band as one power, forgetful of everything other than that we are part of this government, and must be dealt with as men receiving all the rights and privileges of citizenship." She hoped to convince the public that "we must strike now."

It took courage, given the racial climate of the times, for women especially to insist upon recognition of legal rights. In their efforts to secure these rights, the women, of course, had the assistance of men, notably a small group of black lawyers. Among them, for example, was State Senator Robert Brokenburr, who became the second president of the Indianapolis NAACP. These lawyers assisted in bringing cases of discrimination before the courts.

Since 1885 there had been a civil rights law in the Indiana statutes. It prohibited the denial of service or discrimination on account of race in places of public accommodation. The law was largely ignored—it was practically a dead letter. When an occasional suit was brought, the plaintiff nearly always lost the case. One of the first cases instituted by the Indianapolis NAACP was brought by a young female schoolteacher. She had suffered from two alleged violations of the law. A theater had refused to sell her a ticket, and she had been barred from entering Fairview Park (present site of Butler University) as a member of a group, even though the group went to the park as a part of a nature study course which she was required to take to fulfill a teaching requirement.

Even with all the legal setbacks, the NAACP remained at the vanguard in efforts against racial discrimination. The struggle begun by that little group of women in 1912 has been long and has been marked more frequently by failures and frustrations than by victories, but a handful of men and women persisted.

Women never again monopolized the offices of the Indianapolis branch of the NAACP as they did in the first two years, but women have continued over the years to hold offices and to occupy positions of responsibility. A number of the presidents have been women. As other branches of the NAACP were organized throughout the state, women frequently served as officers.

Over the years, the NAACP has championed many efforts to secure racial equality and eliminate discrimination. Women have participated in all of them.

During the years of the Second World War and afterwards, Indiana's black citizens became aroused as never before over the indignities and discrimination to which they were subjected. A group of singularly able people, mostly from the Indianapolis NAACP, mobilized to eliminate Jim Crow practices that still prevailed in restaurants, theaters, and parks in violation of Indiana law. But their most publicized and significant effort was the elimination of legalized segregation in the public schools. Women played an important part in all these efforts and a crucial role in the events that finally culminated in the repeal of the school segregation law in 1949. Incidentally, Indiana was one of the few northern states with such a law and the last northern state to repeal its segregation law.

The school law did not absolutely require segregation but left the policy to the local school authorities. In Indianapolis by the 1920s the policy had become one of complete segregation even though this meant that black children frequently had to be transported long distances out of their neighborhoods and past several white schools. Resentment against this policy had been mounting for some time. Especially because of changing residential patterns, black schools were overcrowded, while in many white schools there were vacant seats.

Things began to happen in the 1940s when Roselyn Richardson's small son was ready to enter school. The Richardsons lived in a neighborhood where the white population was declining, with the result that the enrollment in the white school in the district had declined greatly. Nevertheless, black children were required to travel to a segregated school. Richardson, a very dynamic woman, herself a trained social worker and the wife of a lawyer and former member of the state legislature, attempted to enroll her son in the neighborhood school. She and another black mother who also tried to enroll her child were rebuffed when they appealed to the superintendent of schools. As a result, the women began a campaign through the network of churches, women's clubs, and informal ties to mobilize the black community to insist upon ending segregation in the Indianapolis schools. The NAACP was deeply involved. Unsuccessful efforts were made to elect black members to the Indianapolis

School Board and to influence the board. The NAACP also began to make plans for a court case, but ultimately efforts were concentrated on the state legislature to bring about repeal of the state law that permitted segregation.

Women played an important part in the lobbying efforts that finally culminated in the school law of 1949, which legally abolished segregation in Indiana schools. Most notable was the work of Jessie Jacobs. A graduate of Butler University with a degree in economics and business, Jacobs was active in civic affairs and Republican politics as well as the NAACP. She served as president of the Indianapolis branch of the NAACP and also as president of the state conference. In 1944 she sought election to the state legislature—the first black woman in the history of the state to seek the office. She was a registered lobbyist, working for various causes, including the rights of black students to live in dormitories at Indiana and Purdue universities. She played a key role in the coalition of the NAACP, black civic organizations, interracial church groups, and labor organizations that lobbied effectively and successfully for the 1949 school law. Later Jacobs was elected to the Indianapolis School Board.

Civil rights and political action were closely related, as the history of the school law shows. Once the Nineteenth Amendment was adopted, black women began to participate in politics. For many years, political organizations, like most institutions in Indiana, were racially segregated. There was a state Negro division and speakers bureau, etc., of the Republican and Democratic parties. Women were active in both parties at the local level, but few of them were nominated for public office. The first black woman to be elected to the Indiana General Assembly was Daisy Riley Lloyd, a Democrat elected in 1964. In 1966 Harriet Bailey Conn was elected. She was a most remarkable woman. Her interest in securing legal rights for blacks was undoubtedly inspired by the example of her father, Robert L. Bailey, one of the most significant civil rights lawyers in the history of the state and an important figure in the early history of the NAACP. By the time Conn graduated from law school, she was the mother of seven children as well as being a leader in civic affairs. In addition to serving in the legislature, where she sponsored legislation to increase the rights of women, she became public defender for the state of Indiana and chairman of the Indiana Advisory Committee to the United States Commission on Civil Rights. She was also one of the first black members of the Indianapolis Bar Association.

There have been several black women members of the Indiana House in recent years. One of them was Julia Carson, elected in 1972. As a member of the House, she showed a special interest in issues of concern to women, especially poor women. Carson sponsored a minimum wage law for domestic workers and worked for the Equal Rights Amendment. In 1976 Carson became the first black woman elected to the state Senate.

For many educated black women today, racial barriers have been lowered, if not completely eliminated. But even today, these successes have frequently been achieved against great odds. The general public should not be misled by these well-publicized examples, because these success stories are the exception rather than the rule. In some respects the gap between black women at the top and the majority of black women is widening. As pointed out earlier, for the population as a whole, black women are still the lowest paid and the most exploited of all groups.

In conclusion, the successful women whom I mentioned need no reminder that the successes of today rest on the patient, unselfish, oftentimes unrewarded and largely forgotten efforts of earlier generations of anonymous black women whom history has overlooked.

(This lecture was presented at the Indianapolis Museum of Art in March 1982.)

In Retrospect: The Black Women in the Middle West Project at the Indiana Historical Society

Wilma L. Gibbs

During the 1970s the Indianapolis Section of the National Council of Negro Women (NCNW) collected materials about the lives of black women in Indiana. Unsolicited, two members of that organization, schoolteachers Virtea Downey and Shirley Herd, delivered the materials to Darlene Clark Hine, a Purdue University faculty member. Hine used much of the material in the publication, *When the Truth Is Told: A History of Black Women's Culture and Community in Indiana, 1875–1950,* written in 1981.

The relationship between Hine, Downey, and Herd was the impetus for the Black Women in the Middle West (BWMW) Project. The project was an effort to collect manuscript and photographic records of black women in Illinois and Indiana. In 1982 Hine, an associate professor of history and vice provost at Purdue University, wrote a planning grant for the project, which was funded by the Division of Special Services of the National Endowment for the Humanities (NEH). During the 1982–83 planning year, a small staff, including a project director, administrator, typist, and graduate assistant, enlisted the help of archivists, librarians, academicians, and hundreds of grass-roots volunteers. The year was spent developing an organizational structure, devising a conference workshop, and preparing a proposal to submit to NEH for funds to implement the project.

Initially, the project was to last three years and was to cover a five-state area. The NEH funded the project with a few major revisions: the project was to last eighteen months, and the five-state area, including Illinois, Indiana, Michigan, Ohio, and Wisconsin, was chiseled to two states. The project staff chose Illinois and Indiana. Also, the idea for a black women's history traveling exhibit with an interpretive catalog was abandoned. Additionally, the project was funded at $150,000 ($200,000 had been requested for the five-state project) with the stipulation that a codirector for archives be added to the staff.

An executive committee comprised of a cross section of archivists, librarians, academicians, other professsionals, and nonprofessionals from all five original states was appointed. The committee helped generate local support for the project, reviewed project plans, and aided with the implementation of the grant proposal.

The most important groups of the project were probably the regional committees. The role of these committees, located in key cities throughout both states, was to serve as a forum for the many volunteers. Each committee had a chair who coordinated its work and served as a liaison between the group and the BWMW project central office. The chairs formed the Committee of Regional Coordinators. These committees made contact with people at area libraries and historical societies from whom they could seek advice as they collected records.

Press releases and direct mailings were used to recruit volunteers for the project. Announcements about the project appeared in newspapers, professional journals, and newsletters of selected organizations and historical societies; e.g., numerous articles appeared in *Black History News & Notes*. The newsletter announced the funding of the NEH grant and the conference workshops and meetings. It also provided brief updates of the project. The rate of participation increased as the program narrowed its focus to target the two-state area. Whereas an initial national mailing elicited the support of a group of people who had shown an interest in black women's history (e.g., the Association of Black Women Historians and conferees at two black women's history workshops), later mailings were sent to a more general audience. More nonhistory professionals became involved as the project progressed. According to Hine, this was due to two main factors: 1) tighter control; and 2) wider use of personal appeals that reached women who were involved in church and civic work and club and union activities.

During the planning year, three site visits to Detroit, Madison (Wisconsin), and Chicago were made to gather input from potential participants. The visits were used to fine-tune the project. In Detroit the Task Questionnaire, geared toward potential donors, was thoroughly discussed and refined. Visits to the other two sites clarified the record-collecting focus of the project and helped to revise a BWMW conference/workshop that was held during the spring semester at Purdue University. Letters of inquiries and personal referrals were used to identify potential donors. Women's organizations and individuals were sent solicitations. Most of the referrals came from project participants.

The conference/workshop at Purdue served as a training ground for the collecting aspect of the project. Four instructional sessions focusing on collection were presented at the workshop.

Courtesy of Shirley Herd

Black Women in the Middle West Project personnel included Shirley Herd, community relations consultant; Patrick Bidelman, codirector for administration; Darlene Clark Hine, project director; and Virtea Downey, church relations consultant.

> Session I focused on techniques for getting in touch with potential donors and taking physical possession of records. Participants were encouraged to be sensitive to donors' reservations and fears about releasing their records.
>
> Session II demonstrated how taped interviews could supplement the documentary process.
>
> Session III taught participants how to transport, store, record, and annotate records.
>
> Session IV reviewed the planned working relationship between libraries and archives and the participants.

The implementation phase of the project lasted from January 1984 through June 1985. Eight major conference/workshops were held throughout the summer of 1984. The purpose of these meetings was to train volunteer project representatives to become field-workers in their local communities. Project participants were kept informed through a series of progress reports.

The Indiana Historical Society was one of five repositories that agreed to house the project's collections. The other cooperating institutions, all of which worked closely with the project and supplied an archivist to serve on the Archival Advisory Committee, were the Chicago Historical Society, the Illinois State Historical Society, the Calumet Regional Archives in Gary, and the Northern Indiana Historical Society in South Bend.

BWMW Collections at the Society

The Black Women in the Middle West Project collections at the Society can be divided into two categories. They are the administrative files of the project and the collections of individuals and groups. The administrative files include twenty-eight manuscript boxes, over half of which contain biographical materials related to the project collectors. These files contain the NEH applications and correspondence, general correspondence, mailing lists, project forms and printed matter, and publicity material. Also included are materials arranged topically from various institutions—particularly historical societies and cultural agencies.

The four dozen other collections at the Society that were donated as a direct result of the project reflect a wide range of black women's activity in Indiana. The majority of the collections relate to the lives of individual women or women's organizations. A few collections, such as Starling James's collection of the Federation of Associated Clubs, Mattie Coney's Citizens Forum, and the National Association of Negro Musicians, which includes material related to the Indianapolis Music Promoters, demonstrate women working within coed groups.

The collections range from one item to several cubic feet. Most of the BWMW materials at the Society pertain to central Indiana. More specifically, a representation of women as church workers can be seen in the collections of Alta Jett, Richmond, and Virtea Downey, Indianapolis. They collected materials from churches within their respective cities. Women as civic and organization workers can be seen in the Woman's Improvement Club and Sisters of Charity collections; as family members through the papers of Frances Patterson and Jean Spears; as workers or laborers through the papers of nurse Pauline Eans; as volunteers from the documentation provided by the Alice Tinsley Collection; as educators through the donated collections of Emma L. Chester and Maenell Newsome; as musicians in the papers of lyric soprano Mary L. Dethridge; and as ministers through the papers of Rev. Hester Greer, including her unpublished autobiography.

Evaluating the Project

The Black Women in the Middle West Project at the Society was a valuable endeavor from several vantage points. The project made the Society a more visible entity within the community. It introduced the institution to a whole new group of people, while giving them a greater awareness of the importance of primary source materials in researching and reporting history. Coupled with that, the project emphasized the importance of retrieving material from basements and attics and making it available for researchers at local institutions.

As a public relations tool, the project's limits seem almost boundless both geographically and physically. The first collection lead that I received after arriving at the Society in September 1986 was from a woman who had been very active with the project. She had donated her family papers and had encouraged others to give materials. A former schoolteacher, she was very active in the community, and her contacts proved valuable for future collection leads. Intermittently over the past three years, I have been approached by people who were directly or peripherally involved with the project. Two octogenarians recently contacted me about their concerns that the past be saved for posterity. One woman owned a business in Indianapolis for over fifty years; the other is the daughter of a renowned artist.

During February 1987 the *New York Times* published an article about the project. Sprinkled with observations attributed to director Darlene Clark Hine, the article presented an overview of the project. It was picked up by several newspapers around the country. A onetime Indianapolis resident, Oscar James Fox, read the story in the *Cleveland Plain Dealer.* Fox, who had worked from 1945 to 1960 as a photographer and display technician for Flanner House, a social-service agency that has been active in Indianapolis since 1898, contacted the Society and offered to loan his negatives for copying. In addition to photographing Flanner House activities and events, Fox also captured street scenes in the surrounding area. In particular, his photographic views of several blocks of Indiana Avenue, a once-thriving cultural boulevard, have provided graphic support to a few articles and media shows. It is obvious that an assessment of the project must also include results that are not always measurable in immediate or tangible terms.

As the project is assessed, it is important to examine those things that could have been done differently to increase its effectiveness. There are several issues that can be addressed in evaluating the project. As mentioned earlier, the NEH mandated the hiring of a codirector of archives as a stipulation for funding. Although the project advertised and got very close to hiring someone for the position, the job went unfilled. A portion of the void this created was filled by the archival advisory committee. As a liaison between the central office and the participating institutions, a codirector of archives could have stood objectively outside the five institutions while networking between institutions to address issues that directly impacted the project. The codirector could have been available to travel the two-state area (especially to the pockets that were not reached by the participating institutions) to identify the type of material that would be historically useful. That individual could have served as a consultant to the participating institutions as they made collection decisions. Early on, Shirley Herd, who served as the community relations consultant for the project, compiled a publicity kit. It contained numerous suggestions for individuals who served as regional coordinators of the project. A codirector of archives could have constructed a detailed packet for collecting aimed at institutions, regional coordinators, project participants, and potential donors.

The project affirmed the need to assess how the flow of incoming collections can impact upon an institution's policies and procedures. One issue that was not considered fully was the loaning and copying of materials. In some instances originals may not have been forthcoming, but in many cases, copies were probably too readily accepted. As collections were received there were several access issues. How should collections be named and grouped? What linkage mechanisms should be used to identify collections that resulted from the project? In retrospect, the project stressed the importance of the paper trail from accessioning to processing.

Conclusion

The Black Women in the Middle West Project has served as a prototype for other large-scale collecting efforts that plan to involve lay persons. Recently, representatives of the Armenian Women's Project in Berkeley, California, contacted the Society about a collection project they were planning. They requested and were sent materials from the administrative files of the BWMW collection. Before the collection project, the conditions of black women were best discovered by examining the collections of black men at the Society. However, few of these collections depicted the women's daily lives. Historian Juliet E. K. Walker notes in an essay at the beginning of the Black Women in the Middle West Project guidebook, "as the black historical

Published by the Indiana Historical Bureau

experience moved into the mainstream of American historiography, African-American women's history all too often paralleled white women's history in conceptualization, emphasis, and interpretation. It has been a history of the activities and national achievements of women whose papers have been accessible for scrutiny." Deborah Gray White, in her article "Mining the Forgotten: Manuscript Sources for Black Women's History," expands on these limitations when she discusses access issues for uncovering black women's materials.

In the past few years several articles have been written that utilized collections from the project. They include a broad range of subjects: Lillian Thomas Fox, an early Indianapolis journalist; the Phyllis Wheatley Young Women's Christian Association; pre–Civil War black rural communities; and the Woman's Improvement Club's work with tuberculosis. By examining minute books, journals, diaries, program booklets, and correspondence, these articles have provided new perspectives for scholarship in black women's history.

The Black Women in the Middle West Project was unique. It called upon historians, archivists, and the public at large to cooperate and address the lack of available materials for researching the history of black women. It was one bold footstep on the road to historical accuracy in Indiana and Illinois.

Cities and Rural Communities

Black Rural Settlements in Indiana before 1860

Xenia E. Cord

Indiana prior to the Civil War developed into a haven for the resettlement of free blacks and recently manumitted slaves. However harsh the laws of Indiana were (and throughout the decades of the 1830s and 1840s they were increasingly restrictive), Indiana still represented a part of the country where slavery was forbidden by law. And so, in increasing numbers, free blacks settled in Indiana, aided in large measure by the Society of Friends. When they came they entered land in the public domain, established homesteads in the way of pioneer settlers throughout the state, and lived in associative settlements relatively unmolested by neighboring white settlers. Census manuscripts indicate that extended, two-parent families were the cultural norm among black rural residents; the Puritan work ethic was the economic model, as it was among white settlers.

A large percentage of the free blacks who came to Indiana prior to 1860 were former residents of North Carolina, as were the Quakers often responsible for their migration. In fact, many came from the northwestern upland counties of Guilford and Randolph, where the Society of Friends was especially strong. Because of a basic conflict between Quaker emancipation of their slaves and state law, manumission societies were formed and funds collected to support the orderly resettlement of black migrants in areas having no restrictions against them. Ohio was the primary resettlement area, but Indiana rapidly followed in importance as North Carolina Quakers, accompanied by their charges and free blacks who were fleeing intolerable conditions, moved onto the frontier.[1]

The first communities were established in the southern tiers of counties below the Ten O'Clock Treaty line and in "the gore," the triangular strip of land along the Ohio border running from Cincinnati to Winchester. As the state was settled toward the north and west other communities developed, some as extensions of earlier colonies, some representing completely new migrations. Those who moved into Indiana often did so in extended interfamilial groups, reestablishing communities that had existed elsewhere.[2]

By 1860 there were more than twenty separate settlements of free blacks in Indiana. Among those that are known to have existed (most are now only memories) are the following: Lyles Station, Roundtree, and Sand Hill communities in Gibson County; Pinkston (also called Colored Freedom) in Dubois County; Lick Creek (possibly also called Paddy's Garden or Little Africa) in Orange County; Seymour and Vallonia in Jackson County; Beck's Mill in Washington County; Underwood, Burnett, and Lost Creek in Vigo County; Beech in Rush County; Greenville, Snow Hill, and Cabin Creek in Randolph County; Roberts in Hamilton County; Weaver in Grant County; Bassett and Rush in Howard County; Huggart in St. Joseph County; and settlements in Bartholomew, Jennings, Franklin, and Henry counties for which the names are unknown. The counties along the Ohio River had black populations, especially in urban areas. In addition, Wayne County had a generally distributed, and very

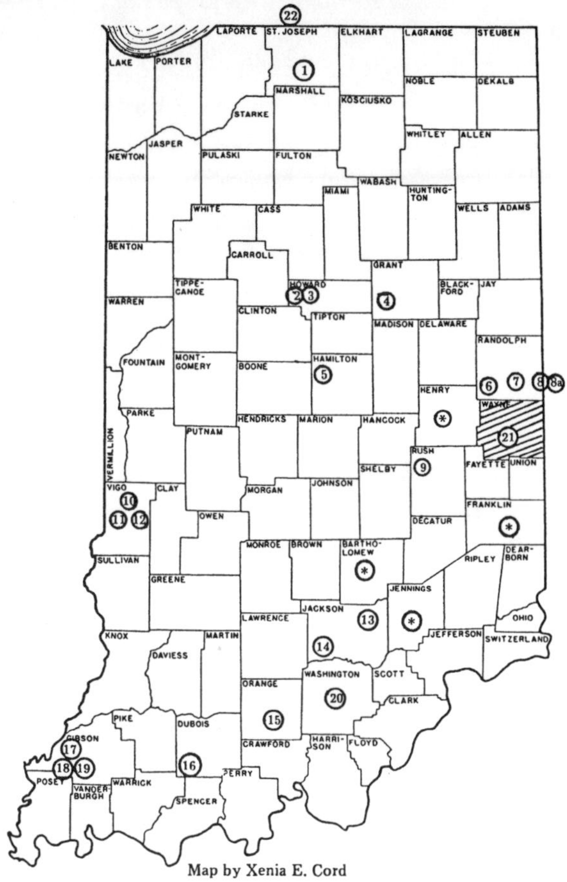

Map by Xenia E. Cord

1 - Huggart, St. Joseph County
2 - Bassett, Howard County
3 - Rush, Howard County
4 - Weaver, Grant County
5 - Roberts, Hamilton County
6 - Cabin Creek, Randolph County
7 - Snow Hill, Randolph County
8 - Greenville, Randolph County
8a - In Darke County, Ohio, the Greenville settlement continued without regard for state boundaries.
9 - Beech, Rush County
10 - Lost Creek, Vigo County
11 - Burnett, Vigo County
12 - Underwood, Vigo County
13 - Seymour, Jackson County
14 - Vallonia, Jackson County
15 - Lick Creek (Little Africa), Orange County
16 - Pinkston (Colored Freedom), Dubois County
17 - Lyles Station, Gibson County
18 - Roundtree, Gibson County
19 - Sand Hill, Gibson County
20 - Beck's Mill, Washington County
21 - Wayne County had a generally distributed, and very large, black population that was apparently not settled into segregated communities, but lived for the most part on land owned by sponsoring or sympathetic Quakers.
22 - Calvin, Cass County, Michigan, was a haven for many Indiana blacks following the Fugitive Slave Law of 1851.
* - Counties which had settlements although names are as yet unknown. See Holmes, "Negro Registers," *Hoosier Genealogist*, 17 (1977), 30-36 and 1850 census data for Greensboro Township, Henry County

large, black population that was apparently not settled into segregated communities, but lived for the most part on land owned by sponsoring or sympathetic Quakers.

Between 1850 and 1860 there had been some shifting in this population; the passage of the Fugitive Slave Law in 1850 resulted in the abandonment of some communities in southern Indiana that were vulnerable to slave catchers and an increase in the population of the more isolated northern settlements. Other blacks fled to the relative security of Michigan and Wisconsin, and a steady stream reached Upper Canada, now called Ontario.

It is likely that the communities that developed along the Wabash River in Knox and Gibson counties were the earliest free black rural settlements in Indiana. Early accounts suggest that most of the African-Americans living in territorial Indiana lived in the Vincennes area, and that emancipated blacks could

IHS C2185

Schoolchildren at Lyles Station, Gibson County, Indiana

be hired for agricultural labor or in conjunction with river traffic on both sides of the Wabash near the settlements of Lyles Station, Sand Hill, and Roundtree.[3]

As early as 1814 Quakers in Washington County were aiding in the resettlement and education of former slaves. Also living in the area were several members of the Roberts family of North Carolina, whose ancestors had been freed since before the American Revolution.[4] Ishmael Roberts bought land in Orange County from the federal reserve in 1824, probably in conjunction with the arrival in that year of Wiley, Nelson, John, and Elias Roberts, who came with their families from North Carolina. By 1850 there were more than 250 black residents of Orange County, among them nine families surnamed Roberts, six named Scott, two families of Duggeds, Burnetts, and Thomases, and families named Chavis, Hawkins, Lynch, Locust, Snead, Chandler, Newby, Weaver, Hatiway, Todd, Hamm, Means, Smith, and Barton.[5]

In the 1820s Robertses also settled in Beech community in Rush County, and when that settlement grew beyond its land capabilities, they moved with neighboring Waldens and Winburns to northern Hamilton County and established a community still known as Roberts Settlement. Other Robertses were among the earliest black settlers in Vigo County. By 1840 William Hill had come from North Carolina to settle in the Rush County community, while his brothers Josiah and Joshua moved further west to Burnett, in Vigo County.[6] Other Beech families were surnamed Watkins, Steward, and Davis.

Roberts Settlement in Hamilton County boasted nearly one hundred residents by 1850, many of them bearing the Roberts surname. According to the Roberts family records, the Hamilton County land was marked off and claimed in 1832 and 1833, and by 1840 eight Roberts families, two Walden families, three Winburn families, and households surnamed Brooks, White, Roads, Sweat, Newsome, Lockleary, Hurley, Rice, Matthews, Guilliams, and Knight had joined the settlement.[7]

In Vigo County the Lost Creek settlement was founded in 1832 by free blacks from North Carolina who had traveled together to the area, having been told by land scout Bowen Roberts of its promise.[8] Among the families traveling together were the Robertses, Stewarts, Chavises, Trevans, Archers, and Andersons. Some of these families lived briefly in Orange County before settling in Vigo County. Other families associated with the Vigo County settlements were Stewart, Artis, and Hawkins.[9]

In the southern Indiana counties where census data suggest that black communities existed but where community names are not known, researchers may use census information and miscellaneous records such as the mandatory Negro registers to determine the location and scope of these settlements. Because of the Fugitive Slave Law and the 1851 Indiana Constitution, black immigrants were required to register and post a bond at their county courthouses. Despite this legal mandate, the diligence with which the registration was pursued seems to have varied around the state. Southern counties were more likely to require registration; however, even in those counties where registries existed, not every black resident registered. In Franklin County, for instance, only 28 of the more than 150 blacks living there in the early 1850s had registered by July 1853.[10] The situation in the county is curious; what caused the exodus is not clear, but by 1860 only 14 blacks still lived there, the rest having scattered to communities farther north.

In Jennings County 213 blacks were counted in the 1850 census, and nearly half of them had registered themselves at the courthouse by late 1853. Among them were these surnames: Anthony, Brandon, Carsey, Dennis, Dunlap, Dye, Edwards, Evans, Harper, Henderson, Henry, Hill, Hood, Hullam, Johnson, King, Lee, McCoppin, Newby, Newsom, Norman, Pettiford, Phillips, Stafford, Valentine, Vickery, Wallace, and White.[11] In Bartholomew County 58 of just over 100 black residents registered (5 of whom were actually from Johnson County) in

1853 and 1854. Among them they represented 15 different surnames.[12]

In Wayne and neighboring Randolph counties the situation was a little different. Both counties were heavily populated by members of the Society of Friends and had large, often transient, black populations whose support and encouragement was a part of the Quaker philosophy. Many black families who later moved to settlements where they were independently domiciled spent their first years in Indiana living on the property, and under the protection, of Quaker families in Wayne and Randolph counties.[13] Because of this arrangement they were often not recorded in the decennial census reports except by numbers.

In 1850 Wayne County had just over twelve hundred black residents. Excluding those who clustered around and in Richmond, most of them lived in New Garden Township, home of Levi Coffin of the Underground Railroad fame, or around the farming communities west of Richmond along the National Road. The numbers remain almost unchanged in 1860, but family and other accounts from black settlers in communities to the north and west make it clear that the 1860 figures represent different people.[14] Black families migrating to Indiana often lived a year or more with Quaker sponsors before moving on to their own settlements, and they were soon replaced by other newcomers.

Randolph County, lying just north of Wayne, was a vital link in the eastern branch of the Underground Railroad and was the location of three large black communities. Cabin Creek and Snow Hill each had over one hundred residents. The Greenville settlement, lying along the Ohio-Indiana line, was actually part of a sprawling rural community located in Randolph County, Indiana, and in Darke County, Ohio, without regard for political boundaries.

Greenville and Cabin Creek were founded about 1822, and Snow Hill was established about fifteen years later.[15] Among the surnames prominent in the area were Lewis, Alexander, Randle, Roberts, Stokes, Burden, Goens, Clemens, Robbins, Outland, Scott, Ward, Skipworth, Moore, Watkins, Shoecraft, Weaver, Bolden, Jones, Quinn, Benson, Chavous [Chavis, Shavers], Demory, and McKeon.[16]

Many of the families who lived first in Wayne County or in the Randolph County communities migrated later to the Weaver settlement in southwestern Grant County. It was founded in the late 1840s when a Quaker named Betts settled the families of Billy Clark, John Wright, Robert Smith, Robert Brazelton, and Robert Brown outside of Jonesboro. By 1860 there were 285 residents of Weaver, including seven families of that name, five named Burden, five named White, three each of Hill and Smith, two Pettiford families, and two Wards, as well as families named Jones, Gulliford, Artis, Becks, and others.[17] Others moved north and west to Howard County, one of the last counties in the state to be organized. The Bassett and Rush communities in Howard County were both small, totaling no more than thirty families at their peak. Among them were six Bassett families, three Artis families, three named Rush, two Hardimon brothers and their families, and families named Gregg, Kennedy, West, Harvey, Harrington, and Ellis.[18]

The Huggart settlement of St. Joseph County was a single surname community, but it points the way to Cass County, Michigan, just across the state line from St. Joseph County, where there was a very large black settlement in the town of Calvin.[19] A great many of the free blacks who had lived in Indiana communities before the Civil War moved to Cass County out of fear of the slave catchers emboldened by the Fugitive Slave Law, or because Michigan represented a safer haven or greater opportunity.

As a final note, the communities in Indiana that were well established by 1860 were composed to a large degree of people of racially mixed heritage. Many had white and Indian ancestors, and often it was the white ancestry that had resulted in their freedom and migration. A number of the families have founding legends pointing to their African royal background or Indian ancestry, or attesting to their perpetual free status. Within communities the families tended to intermarry, since in rural Indiana before 1860 opportunities for free socialization with potential marriage partners from other areas was infrequent.

There was, however, a loosely organized and far-flung interfamily relationship evident among the communities. There is plenty of evidence that these settlers were acquainted and had familial, cultural, and economic ties, both in their home states

IHS C4595

Although most of the black rural communities have vanished, many thrived through the early part of the twentieth century. Eli Archey farmed at Beech Settlement, Rush County, Indiana, ca. 1910.

and after resettling in Indiana. Surnames recur with frequency, as demonstrated in this brief review, and movement and communication between families and settlements occurred. Certain external factors tended to unite the communities. Participation in the slave-smuggling activities of the Quakers connected the settlements, as did the visits of circuit-riding black ministers. Also, the black convention movement, especially as it sought educational opportunities for black children, allied the communities.

Today most of these settlements have vanished from the landscape, but emotional and kinship ties continue to re-create the communities. A number hold annual reunions, often called Homecomings, either on a family, a community, or a church congregation basis.[20] Members of some of these organizations have become self-appointed historians of the settlements from which they are descended, collecting oral histories, documents, photographs, genealogies, and artifacts from descendants and publishing histories.

Federal census reports, manuscripts, abstracts, some of the county histories, and publications of the Indiana Historical Society and its Black History Program are extremely useful resources for the beginning researcher. Anyone researching the history of the black settlements of Indiana quickly becomes aware of the paucity of reliable material and of its scattered and esoteric nature. A great deal still needs to be done to record and to understand fully the significance of this unique aspect of Indiana history.

Notes

1. For background information on migration and resettlement in Indiana, see James H. Boykin, *The Negro in North Carolina Prior to 1861* (New York: Pageant Press, Inc., 1958); William E. Farrison, "The Negro Population of Guilford County, North Carolina, before the Civil War," *North Carolina Historical Review* 21 (Oct. 1944): 319–29; John Hope Franklin, *The Free Negro in North Carolina, 1790–1860* (Chapel Hill: University of North Carolina Press, 1943) and "The Free Negro in the Economic Life of Ante-Bellum North Carolina," *North Carolina Historical Review* 19 (July–Oct. 1942): 239–59, 358–75; Rosser Howard Taylor, *The Free Negro in North Carolina* (Chapel Hill:

University of North Carolina Press, 1920); *A Narrative of Some of the Proceedings of North Carolina Yearly Meeting on the Subject of Slavery within Its Limits* (Pamphlet, Greensboro, N.C., 1846).

2. The Roberts family migrations, from North Carolina to Orange, Rush, Vigo, and Hamilton counties, can be pieced together through such sources as Wanda G. Williams, "Negro Count Was Taken," and "Page in History Is Uncovered; Little Africa Cemetery Found," *Bloomington Herald-Times,* 3 Jan. 1971; Nathan Hill, "Beech Settlement," *Indiana Negro History Society Bulletin* (May 1943), unpaged; Paul Anderson, Beulah Ross, and June Love, "Lost Creek Settlement, Vigo County, Indiana," ibid. (Mar. 1938), unpaged; Stephen Vincent, "Roberts Settlement: The Forming of a Successful Black Rural Community" (Unpublished honors thesis, Indiana University, 1980).

3. Reliable data on early free black residents is difficult to find. See Emma Lou Thornbrough, *The Negro in Indiana before 1900: A Study of a Minority,* vol. 37 of *Indiana Historical Collections* (Indianapolis: Indiana Historical Bureau, 1957), 22 n. 33, for 1810 statistics on Knox County, out of which Gibson County was formed. The 1820 manuscript census for Gibson County lists seventy-five "colored" residents, of whom eighteen females and twelve males were "bound to service." The remaining forty-five were free. Among these was Phillip Sumner, a blacksmith, who may have been one of the slaves emancipated and resettled on land purchased in 1816 by Thomas E. Sumner of Nollensville, Tennessee. Carl C. Lyles, Sr., *Lyles Station Yesterday and Today* (Evansville, Ind.: Burkert-Walton, Inc., 1984), deals with a slightly later period, but George Flower, *History of the English Settlement in Edwards County, Illinois, Founded in 1817 and 1818, by Morris Birkbeck and George Flower* (Chicago: Fergus Printing Co., 1882), 257–72, suggests that commerce between Illinois and Indiana was common; he also mentions (p. 266) that during the War of 1812 William Henry Harrison mustered a company of blacks to protect the frontier.

4. For reference to some early records see Isabel Boyer, "Quaker Meetinghouse Puts Tiny Area on Map," *Indianapolis Star,* 13 Nov. 1982, concerning Quakers from Elizabeth City, North Carolina, who came to Indiana in 1814 with their emancipated slaves. Settling in Washington County, they were members of the Blue River Quarterly Meeting, which established an academy attended by black children. A related source is "An Account Book of the Indiana Yearly Meeting of Friends Committee on the Concerns of the People of Color, 30 September 1835 to 14 August 1841," a manuscript located at the Lilly Library, Indiana University, Bloomington. It mentions payments to the Springboro Monthly Meeting for books for the "colored school," and to Blue River Quarterly Meeting for its academy. The Roberts family of neighboring Orange County boasted at least two Revolutionary War veterans, Ishmael Roberts and Thomas Archie, as noted by Williams in "Page in History."

5. Williams, "Negro Count Was Taken"; "Population of Civil Divisions Less than Counties, Table III—State of Indiana," in United States Bureau of the Census, *The Statistics of the Population of the United States, Ninth Census, 1870,* 3 vols. (Washington, D.C.: Government Printing Office, 1872), 1:122–31, showing totals by county for 1850, 1860, and 1870.

6. Hill, "Beech Settlement."

7. Edgar C. Conkling, "Roberts Settlement: A Mixed Blood Agricultural Community in Indiana" (Unpublished M.A. thesis, University of Chicago, 1957), 25.

8. Vincent, "Roberts Settlement," 4. Between 1830 and 1835 Robertses in Indiana engaged in considerable correspondence with relatives in North Carolina. See Anderson, Ross, and Love, "Lost Creek," who attribute this folkloric excerpt to Bowen

Roberts: "Fat hogs are now roaming the forest with knives and forks sticking in their backs."

9. Anderson, Ross, and Love, "Lost Creek."

10. These figures were reached by comparing United States Bureau of the Census, *The Statistics of Population* (1870), 1:124, and a hand count of the 1850 microfilmed manuscript census for Franklin County, with the names listed in Maurice Holmes, "Negro Registers: Bartholomew, Franklin, and Jennings Counties," *The Hoosier Genealogist* 17 (June 1977): 32–33.

11. Holmes, "Negro Registers," 33–36.

12. Ibid., 30–31.

13. Aseneth Peters Artis, "The Negro in Grant County," in Rolland L. Whitson, *Centennial History of Grant County, Indiana*, 2 vols. (Chicago and New York: The Lewis Publishing Co., 1914), 1:349; Cora M. Straughn, ed., *"Lest We Forget": Reminiscences of the Pioneers of Grant County, Indiana* (Marion, Ind.: Marion High School History Department, 1921), unpaged.

14. Artis, "The Negro in Grant County"; Straughn, ed., *"Lest We Forget,"* and taped oral interviews with Helen Pettiford Artis, 8 Aug. 1980; Fred Beck and Delores Beck Betts, 21 Nov. 1980; and Cassius Pettiford and Helen Pettiford Artis, 20 Aug. 1980, in the author's collection.

15. Ebenezer Tucker, *History of Randolph County, Indiana* (Chicago: A. L. Kingman, 1882), 133–34.

16. Ibid., 133–41. A little-known government document, on 348 rolls of microfilm, is "Eastern Cherokee Applications of the United States Court of Claims, 1906–1909," and the 12 rolls recording "Records Relating to Enrollment of Eastern Cherokees by Guion Miller, 1908–1910," in which descendants of free blacks in North Carolina who lived in Randolph, Grant, and Howard counties (primarily) at the turn of the century claimed Cherokee ancestry in order to participate in the federal compensation program. Although uniformly rejected because they did not fulfill requirements of having an ancestor previously recorded as Cherokee, their claims and the subsequent investigations provide a wealth of genealogical data and ample evidence of the interrelationships existing among the communities.

17. Artis, "The Negro in Grant County"; hand count of the manuscript census records (on microfilm) for Liberty Township, Grant County, in 1860; Xenia E. Cord, "Stand Fast in Liberty: A Study of a Black Rural Community [Weaver, Indiana]" (Unpublished graduate paper, Indiana University, 1981).

18. Wayne Guthrie, "When Did Bassett, Rush Fade Away?," *Indianapolis News*, 11 Aug. 1953; Dawne Slater, "Bassetts Prominent in Ervin Township," and "Blacks Often Settled Near Friends," *Kokomo Tribune*, 23 Feb. 1986; C. V. Haworth, taped interview, 12 Jan. 1966, Kokomo-Howard County Public Library Tape File, Kokomo, Indiana.

19. Frederick A. Karst, "A Rural Black Settlement in St. Joseph County, Indiana, before 1900," *Indiana Magazine of History* 74 (Sept. 1978): 252–67. For Cass County, Michigan, see George K. Hesslink, *Black Neighbors: Negroes in a Northern Rural Community* (Indianapolis: Bobbs-Merrill Co., 1968); Richard M. Dorson, *Negro Tales from Pine Bluff, Arkansas, and Calvin, Michigan* (Bloomington: Indiana University Press, 1958).

20. "Beech Homecoming," *Black History News & Notes* (Oct. 1980): 1; Reginald Bishop, "Roberts Heritage Rich," *Indianapolis News*, 2 Feb. 1976; Xenia E. Cord, "Generations: The Pettiford/Weaver Homecoming" (Unpublished graduate paper, Indiana University, 1980), and "Homecoming: The Pettiford Family Reunion," an unedited videotape in the author's collection.

The *Evansville Argus* and Black Evansville, 1938–1943

Darrel E. Bigham

The understanding of African-American history in Indiana is made enormously richer by the handful of black newspapers published in the state during the past ninety or so years. The most well known paper is, of course, the *Indianapolis Recorder.* Virtually unknown is the *Evansville Argus,* a weekly that appeared from June 1938 until October 1943. The first black newspaper in the Crescent City to last beyond a few issues and the most long-lived among the few that appeared, the *Argus* provided a unique perspective on Evansville during the latter part of the New Deal and the first half of the Second World War. An examination of the paper, a full set of which has been preserved in the Special Collections Department of the University of Southern Indiana, offers much insight into what was one of the most eventful periods in the history of black Evansville. It also allows one to appreciate the difficulties faced by black newspaper publishers. Despite the short life of the *Argus,* the paper provided an important legacy of ideas, ideals, and leaders.[1]

In 1938 black Evansville remained mired in a legacy of over seventy years of blatant racial discrimination. Not surprisingly, the three daily newspapers in the 1930s tended to focus on unflattering aspects of black society—racial stereotypes and crime, notably—and reinforced racial segregation by separate obituary sections and by classified advertisements with "white" and "colored" labels. Some progress was being made, however, primarily as a result of federal programs. The city's first public housing project, Lincoln Gardens, opened in July 1938 on the site of what had once been the heart of Baptistown (the name commonly used for the heart of the black community since the 1890s). Blacks also benefited from a wide range of educational and occupational programs offered by the Works Progress Administration (WPA). In addition, the local chapter of the National Association for the Advancement of Colored People (NAACP) was revived after twenty years of inactivity in 1938. Two issues were particularly important to the group—the sentencing to death of a young black for the murder of a white grocer and the opening of a segregated public vocational high school. When defense preparedness became important in 1940, the NAACP also championed equal opportunity in employment.[2]

In this setting the *Evansville Argus* appeared on 25 June 1938. The general manager, Julius W. Holder, urged all black Evansvillians to patronize the paper, which he declared would serve all the people of the city, tell the truth, fight for progress, and "never tolerate injustice or corruption." An advisory committee of five black leaders, including the manager of Lincoln Gardens and the principal of Lincoln High School, was announced. Initially the paper was published in the front room of Mrs. Ida Jones's home on Mulberry Street.[3] Subsequently it opened an office at 609–611 South Elliott Street. The *Argus* sought a new agenda for black Evansville. Instead of the "filthy lucer [*sic*] that is passed during election time," Holder envisioned a community center, a swimming pool, a golf course, greater employment opportunities, a health clinic, better appointments in city and country government, a "race spokesman," and a "new out-

MEDICAL ASSOCIATION MEETS HERE JUNE 28-29

COVERING EVANSVILLE AND ADJOINING TERRITORY

THE EVANSVILLE ARGUS

HOME OWNED HOME OPERATED

VOL. 1—NO. 1 EVANSVILLE, INDIANA, SATURDAY, JUNE 25, 1938

JAMES SWAIN FACES ELECTRIC CHAIR JULY 1

Six Colored Train Employes Are Hurt In Wreck Disaster

Local Dentist Elected President of Medical Ass'n

Prominent Doctor Is Honored By Outpost

NAACP Hold Meet Sunday

POPULAR MATRON

SERVES LOCAL "Y" AS DIRECTOR FOR 14 YEARS

TEACHER HURT IN AUTO CRASH

BIKE CLUB ENJOYS SUNDAY RIDE

KKK Emblem In Act To Scare Negro Workers

HARLEM WAS FIGHT CRAZY

Mammoth Ins. Co. Celebrates 23rd Anniversary

Powers of Tennis Enter N.C. Tourney

ASBURY RESIGNS AS DOWNINGTOWN SEC'Y

SUFFERS DEFEAT

LOCAL TAP ROOM POPULAR WITH PLEASURE SEEKERS

Fight Probe Tense

Local Boy On Indiana State Tennis Team

Ozzie Simmons On Job

First Negro Graduate of Univ. of Md. Law Dept.

GIRLS VISITING CITY LOST SEVERAL HOURS

JOE LOUIS SUES FIRM FOR $25,000 DAMAGES

Child Falls 2 Floors

Three Colored Essayists Win International Prizes

The first issue of the Evansville Argus *appeared on 25 June 1938.*

Courtesy of University of Southern Indiana Special Collections/University Archives

look." Seven thousand Evansville blacks, he insisted, desired intelligent and civic-minded leadership, which could come only with a better-educated clergy, fewer churches, more intraracial cooperation, and a stronger black business community.[4]

To achieve that end, Holder was as critical of blacks for their lethargy and parochialism as he was of white racism. In an editorial, "Are You Satisfied?," published on 11 March 1939, he asserted, "I could caption this editorial: FOR SALE—9,000 [*sic*] Spineless Creatures—and feel free in doing so."[5] He also noted that it was unfair to criticize the efforts of the *Argus* by comparing it with the *Recorder* or the *Pittsburgh Courier,* since Evansville's black community was much smaller and its people poorer and less inclined to support new ideas. In August 1941 though, Holder praised his readers for their support of his efforts, which had produced three years of uninterrupted publication "out in the deep, deep blue of fighting for the rights of the minority group in the city."[6]

Little is known about the background of Julius W. Holder, who, after arriving in the city in 1938, held various titles with the *Argus*—general manager, editor, and publisher. There are no records of the establishment or dissolution of the paper in local city or county offices. Internal evidence reveals that, given the title of the paper and the amount of coverage of St. Louis and East St. Louis blacks, Holder had strong ties to the St. Louis region. Holder was also an outspoken Republican and a member of the Roman Catholic church. The *Argus* staff was small: in November 1939 there were, besides Holder, a circulation manager, two advertising managers, a society editor, and a sports reporter. Compensation was undoubtedly modest for the staff, and turnover was frequent. The most continuous service was provided by Charles "Dusty" Decker, Congress of Industrial Organizations (CIO) official and semiprofessional softball player, who wrote on a variety of subjects. In 1943 Holder married society editor, Marylynn Moorman, who also served as secretary to the manager of Lincoln Gardens.[7]

From the outset the newspaper contained three types of stories—releases from the *St. Louis Argus,* correspondence from reporters in local clubs and churches, and local news, written chiefly by Holder and Decker. The amount of correspondence from clubs and churches was substantial for the first three years. In 1942 and 1943, however, the volume of local correspondence declined significantly. Releases from the St. Louis paper continued to be published, and stories published by *India News,* which advocated Indian independence, were added. Most of the material on national issues appeared to be canned material from news releases of various groups, not from wire services. News about the local front was increasingly devoid of controversy and dealt instead—as did editorials—with the efforts of black men and women in the armed forces. The only two staff members identified in print were Holder and the society editor.[8]

Circulation and advertising data for the *Argus* are sketchy. Regarding the former, the paper claimed to be the largest and most progressive paper of its kind in southern Indiana. One issue, 7 February 1942, was sold out. In July 1942 the editor claimed that circulation was ten thousand. With respect to the latter, as a rule a third to a half of the space in the paper was devoted to advertising between 1938 and 1942, but by the spring of 1943 the amount of advertising space had dropped to about 25 percent. Without information about the price of ads or total revenue derived therefrom, it is difficult to draw many conclusions, except to note that the amount of space declined over the years and that some ads were placed by white businesses or politicians seeking black support. Locals of the CIO also advertised regularly. A vast majority of the advertisements came from the few black businesses—groceries, bars, and liquor stores—that existed in Baptistown.[9]

The *Argus* pursued the goals announced in June 1938 by encouraging local pride, by seeking to expand the horizons of black Evansvillians, by promoting self-improvement and self-determination, and by attacking segregation, especially in employment and education. The paper promoted pride by, among other things, carrying stories about "firsts" among local and national blacks. The first issue, for instance, carried a story about a state convention of black doctors, dentists, and pharmacists in Evansville—an organization chaired by Dr. William F. Dendy, a resident of the city since 1926. On 13 August 1938 it reprinted an article from the "white daily" of Brazil, Indiana, in which Evansville's black American Legion post was noted as a winner in state Legion competition. In August 1939 it observed that the first black had been appointed as a city electrician—the same man who in 1928 had been named as the city's first black postal clerk. In the summer of 1942 page one of the *Argus* proudly noted that Evansville educator Charles E. Rochelle had become the first black to receive an Ed.D. from the University of California at Berkeley. The hiring of the first black clerk in a Main Street store in April 1943 received similar billing.[10]

The *Argus* sought to expand the horizons of local blacks by covering church and club activities in the city and by providing information about blacks in other parts of the nation. Typical of these stories was a series of local black church histories commenced in October 1938, the lists of patients in the black Welborn-Walker Hospital Annex, and a catalog of WPA programs and activities. During the war the paper featured stories about offerings at the black United Service Organizations (USO) and exploits of local men and women in the service. The *Argus* carried news about the progress of black college and professional teams, of efforts to break down Jim Crow laws, and of federal legislation (like the fate of the WPA), which directly affected black Americans.[11]

In addition, the paper advocated and sometimes initiated projects aimed at self-improvement and self-determination. It took an active part in the drive for a new community center, promoted programs designed to improve the health and living conditions of Evansville blacks, and sponsored cooking schools to assist local women in preparing more nutritious foods for their families. It also held a series of "Miss Evansville *Argus*" contests, which were publicized through the black branch of the public library and the adult classes sponsored by the WPA.[12]

Closely related to these activities was the *Argus*'s promotion of racial self-determination, particularly in the development of businesses in Baptistown. The paper carried prominent stories, for example, about the campaigns of black-owned life insurance companies in the city. It also encouraged blacks to patronize black-owned businesses or stores in which blacks were employed. In the fall of 1938 the paper publicized the efforts of the NAACP to have more blacks hired by firms on Lincoln Avenue. A year later its efforts included support for a boycott of Lincoln Avenue stores—a tactic that produced not only the hiring of five blacks but also vocal opposition from some black clergymen who thought Holder was too militant.[13]

An important means of encouraging self-determination, according to Holder, was the creation of a "race spokesman" (mayor) for "Derbyville"—a new and more attractive name for Baptistown. Traditionally whites had selected a black to represent black Evansville. Holder's idea was that blacks would choose their own spokesman who, with the support of civic organizations, would bring pressure to bear on white leaders. Based on a similar program in Indianapolis, the campaign was launched in April 1939, and a month later Dr. E. M. Baylor, prominent physician and Republican leader, was inaugurated mayor of Derbyville at Lincoln Gardens. A similar campaign was held in the spring of 1940, when Alfred Lambert, active in the local waiters' union, was elected. (Lambert left town for a better job shortly thereafter.) There is no evidence that the plan produced the results Holder desired.[14] No campaigns were held after that, although an effort was made to revive the plan in 1946.

The failure of the Derbyville mayor plan did not thwart other proposals to improve the lot of black Evansvillians. The *Argus* established a "Colored Shoppers' Day" feature in July 1940 in which some Main Street merchants actively solicited black patronage. Most important was the paper's endorsement of the NAACP's attempts to allow blacks to attend the new vocational school, Mechanic Arts. In 1940 and 1941 it played an important part in abortive efforts to desegregate the school, which it declared was a key ingredient in blacks obtaining the many jobs anticipated as a result of defense buildups.[15]

Yet Holder also expressed impatience with local black leaders, whom he credited with perpetuating a community of run-down shacks, inadequate recreational and occupational opportunities, and racially segregated public facilities. He regularly portrayed black clergymen as the root of black Evansville's problems and argued that blacks needed to stop, as he put it, blindly casting their ballots for Democratic candidates. In the fall of 1940, for example, he demonstrated what he meant by housing the Colored Willkie Club in the *Argus*'s office. In the early months of the war he took another step by helping to form the Council of Clubs to promote the local war effort, inform the community about war-related developments, and provide effective leadership for blacks in local civic affairs. Claiming membership of twenty-three organizations, the council joined the attack on the segregated Mechanic Arts School and organized the local "Double-V" campaign—victory over racism at home as well as abroad—which sought not only to sell war bonds but also to improve employment opportunities for blacks in the booming defense plants of the river city. The *Argus* helped to organize the black USO facility in the fall of 1942 after black soldiers at nearby Camp Breckenridge were denied admission to the Evansville USO.[16]

By mid-1943 the efforts of the *Argus* and the NAACP to improve the educational and employment opportunities of blacks had met with little success. The few advances in education—i.e., better night school offerings—occurred within the context of segregated education. A few blacks were upgraded at two local defense plants, Chrysler and Sunbeam, but an overwhelming majority continued to work in unskilled labor and service positions. In addition, wartime social stress—produced by the influx of hundreds of black laborers and soldiers, the inadequacy of recreational facilities, the poor quality and quantity of housing for blacks, and interracial conflict between visiting white soldiers and black natives—received little attention from white leaders.[17]

Perhaps because of limited success in those respects and/or the fact that winning the war seemed to take precedence over all domestic concerns, the tone of the *Argus* shifted markedly by the spring of 1943. Editorials, moreover, rarely dealt with local issues. The newspaper was usually only four pages long and appeared irregularly in the late summer and early fall. The 22 October 1943 issue was the last. No explanation was offered, and the only indication that publication was ceasing was an indirect reference that there were many photographs in the office that interested persons were welcome to take. Holder apparently left town shortly thereafter. He is not listed in the 1944 city directory.[18]

The ending of the *Argus* at the height of wartime activity is curious, especially since the paper was the first and most long-lived in the history of black Evansville. Internal evidence—the decline in typographical quality, the shrinkage of advertising space, the irregularity of publication, the frequent references to the shoestring budget of the paper, and the changes in the tone and scope of news and editorial coverage—offer a clue. Oral history sources suggest that the lack of advertising, especially from black businesses, was the most damaging factor. That was, however, symptomatic of the fact that black Evansville was, by comparison with Indianapolis or Pittsburgh, extremely small, and that, combined with the paucity of black businesses and professional services, meant that the success of a black newspaper was from the outset unlikely. Perhaps wartime stress—newsprint shortages, the loss of staff members to the draft, the departure of men like Alfred Lambert for better jobs in Chicago, and the emphasis on patriotism rather than justice—made success even less likely. Other contributing factors may have been Holder's attacks on local clergymen, his affiliation with the Roman Catholic church, and his open identification with Republican leadership.[19]

The *Argus* provides a fascinating perspective on five of the most important years in the history of black Evansville. Its demise tells much about the realities of life in smaller black communities in Indiana, to be sure, but in the brief course of its history the *Argus* made enormous contributions to the struggle for racial justice in Evansville. In 1946 former staff member Dusty Decker was the first, and only, black elected to the Indiana House from southern Indiana. A number of its efforts—notably the Council of Clubs—survived the war and helped to establish the basis for postwar assaults on Jim Crow laws.

Notes

1. See, for example, Darrel E. Bigham, "Work, Residence, and the Emergence of the Black Ghetto in Evansville, 1865–1900," *Indiana Magazine of History* 76 (Dec. 1980): 287–318.

2. *Evansville Argus,* 25 June, 2, 9 July 1938; 29 Apr., 15 July, 24 Aug. 1939; 19 Apr., 18 Oct. 1940; 11 June 1943.

3. Ibid., 25 June 1938; 1 Aug. 1941.

4. Ibid., 16, 23 July 1938.

5. Ibid., 11 Mar. 1939.

6. Ibid., 9 Apr. 1939; 1 Aug. 1941.

7. Ibid., 25 June 1938; 7 Oct. 1939; 18 Oct. 1940; 27 June 1941; 2 July 1943.

8. Ibid., 9 Apr. 1939; 10 Oct. 1941; 2 Jan., 12 Mar. 1943. See the July through Oct. 1943 issues, passim.

9. Ibid., 3 June, 11 Nov. 1939; 23 May, 15 Nov. 1941; 14 Feb. 1942; 26 Mar., 28 May, 23 July 1943.

10. Ibid., 25 June, 13 Aug. 1938; 17 June, 5, 24 Aug., 21 Oct. 1939; 15 Aug. 1942; 23 Apr. 1943.

11. Ibid., 1 Oct. 1938; 4, 11 Feb. 1939; 19 Apr. 1940; 5 Sept. 1942; 6 Mar., 23 July 1943.

12. Ibid., 2 July, 3 Sept. 1938; 1 Apr. 1939; 5 July 1940; 12 Sept., 24 Oct. 1941.

13. Ibid., 20 Aug., 3, 17 Sept., 8 Oct. 1938; 18 Mar., 9 Apr., 19 Aug., 9 Sept., 7, 21 Oct. 1939; 17, 31 May, 25 Oct., 20 Dec. 1940; 2 May 1941.

14. Ibid., 9 July 1938; 28 Jan., 18 Feb., 25 Mar., 9 Apr., 13 May 1939.

15. Ibid., 14 June, 19 July, 18 Oct., 1 Nov., 20 Dec. 1940.

16. Ibid., 26 July, 25 Oct., 1 Nov. 1940; 31 Jan., 14 Feb., 7 Mar., 11, 18 Apr., 5 Sept., 10 Oct. 1942; 21 May, 11 June, 30 July, 9 Sept., 1 Oct. 1943.

17. Ibid., 9 Sept., 1 Oct. 1943. Max Cavnes, *The Hoosier Community at War,* vol. 9 of *Indiana in World War Two* (Bloomington: Indiana University Press, 1961), 125–27, 140–41.

18. *Evansville Argus,* July–Oct. 1943, passim.

19. Ibid., 16 July 1938; 19 Sept. 1942; 19 Mar., 16 Apr. 1943.

In Pursuit of Full Enjoyment of Liberty and Happiness: Blacks in Antebellum Indianapolis, 1820–1860

Earline Rae Ferguson

The search for a history of antebellum black Hoosiers that would depict their local life, homes, and daily condition is an arduous one. Rarely are blacks mentioned in public records or newspapers of that period. Even more rarely did they leave personal journals and accounts for the researcher. The various town censuses mentioned in nineteenth-century local newspapers and Indianapolis histories did not survive the demolition and moving of city offices to new sites at different times, and thus are not available for study. This makes it difficult to find specific information regarding the early black residents of Indianapolis—if indeed there is such specific information.

The use of sources such as the federal manuscript censuses can help one uncover information about the residential, occupational, educational, and familial patterns of antebellum blacks. Those censuses, however, are neither faultless nor comprehensive and tend to undercount not only blacks but also the poor and the young. Additionally, the information collected by census takers often reflected conditions existing only on the day of their visits, so that individuals who might have lived in Indianapolis in the decade between census takings were not reflected in the tabulations. Also, families or individuals surveyed, who moved from one location to another within the census-taking period, were sometimes counted twice. Finally, the pre-1880 censuses did not provide specific residential information, making it difficult to discern early residential patterns.

Enumerations in pre-1850 surveys conducted by the United States Bureau of the Census do not provide the answers to questions such as who the inhabitants of households actually were, where they came from, what their relationships were, how much property they owned, or what their hopes and aspirations were. It is possible, however, to get a general overview of the number of people residing in Indianapolis prior to 1850 by using a combination of censuses, local histories, and locally published newspapers. None of those sources, however, contains the thoughts and words of blacks. Instead they are based on the white community's perceptions of the lives of blacks in Indianapolis. This study does not pretend to provide a complete picture of the early history of Indianapolis blacks. Rather, it hopefully will present a summary of foundations upon which the rich community life of Indianapolis blacks has been built—the seeds from which the community and its institutions have sprung.[1]

The general attitude in the city of Indianapolis, indeed throughout the state of Indiana, in the antebellum period was antiblack. Black men were not allowed to vote, to serve on juries or in the militia, to testify against a white man, or to send their children to public schools. Indiana did not encourage black settlement. Despite the provision of the Northwest Ordinance of 1787 that forbade slavery and involuntary servitude, the legal status of black Hoosiers was tenuous at best. Prior to 1810 blacks in the Indiana Territory were enslaved in the guise of indentured servitude. In 1803 the territory had passed restrictive legislation providing that blacks could be brought into Indiana only under a system of indenture that required them to serve out their terms, and additionally required their male and female children to serve until the ages of thirty and twenty-eight years, respectively. In 1820 the Indiana Supreme Court recognized that the state constitution of 1816 abolished slavery, but ignored those indentures that were made before 1810. In 1821 the state supreme court outlawed involuntary servitude, but custom dictated that the status of black Hoosiers remain dubious throughout the antebellum period.[2]

Antebellum blacks did not make up a significant portion of the Indianapolis population—never more than 5 percent. Who were those early black Indianapolis residents? According to most Indianapolis histories, the first black to enter the city was Aaron Wallace, the young servant that Gen. John Tipton brought with him when he helped select the site as the new state capital. Wallace's stay, however, was a temporary one, as he left with Tipton. The city's first black resident was Cheney Lively, the housekeeper who accompanied Alexander Ralston, one of the city's planners. After Ralston's death, Lively remained in Indianapolis living on property she owned on Maryland Street. Dr. Samuel G. Mitchell, the town's first doctor, brought another black to Indianapolis—Ephraim Enshaw, a freedman who worked for wages. By 1821 other blacks had settled in Indianapolis, including David Mallory, the town's first barber. By 1836 Indianapolis blacks were clustered on the banks of the canal in an area called "Colored Town."[3]

The fifth United States census reveals that twenty-one Indianapolis households claimed black residents. Seventy-six percent of those households had a white as head of the house. The blacks in those households were probably indentured servants. Under a law passed in 1831, Indiana required blacks entering the state to post a bond of five hundred dollars as security for their good behavior. Failure to do so meant they could be seized and sold to the highest bidder for six months.

Five hundred dollars was an exorbitant amount, so there were many blacks working out their indentures during the antebellum period. Of the remaining households 83 percent had a black male head of house. Cheney Lively was the only black female head of house. No small children lived in her household, just two other unidentified black women. One-half of the male-headed households contained children, indicating the existence of family groups. In one of those households John Partridge lived with his wife and three young daughters. Another household contained James Overall, his wife and young son, another black adult male, and two other black adult females. John Tucker and his wife lived with a young adult male. Sampson Leatherman and his wife kept house for just the two of them. David Mallory was the only black head of household living alone.[4]

James Overall and John Tucker were victims of the violence and lawlessness that characterized antebellum American life. For blacks, particularly, violence was a factor of life. White mobs indiscriminately attacked them, usually in black residential areas and usually focusing on the symbols of black achievement—churches, businesses, or schools. Both Bethel AME and Second Baptist churches were "mysteriously" destroyed by fire during the antebellum period. Tucker and Overall, however, were the victims of more personal attacks. The Overall family lived immediately east of Military Park. Sometime near the end of 1838 an "unruly mob" attacked the family for reasons unknown today, and for which some were "persecuted," but most escaped. On the Fourth of July 1845, however, John Tucker was murdered downtown, reportedly in the presence of two hundred people.[5]

Attacks on antebellum blacks often resulted from white resentment of abolitionist agitation and the perception that the antislavery movement was a threat to white workers. The *Indiana State Sentinel* reported that Tucker, "a steady, unoffensive man, who had purchased his freedom many years ago in Kentucky," was murdered by a gang of men who were drunk from celebrating the Fourth. The *Ohio Anti-Slavery Bugle* reported Tucker was killed

> in the presence of *two hundred people*—multitudinuous voices exclaiming . . . "Kill the d——d nigger, kill him!" *They beat him after he was dead.* And as he lay with the blood bubbling round him, the cry arose for more blood. "The niggers are gitting too thick, and they ought to be thinned out"—"I would as lieve kill a nigger as an ox"—"Damn them—I wish every one was shot, and the Abolitionists too"—were the exclamations which broke from their infuriate lips. No effort was made to stay the mob, though at any moment there was enough of *good society* to arrest the violence.

Although several people were involved in the murder, only one arrest was made. At that point, the mob turned itself on Henry De Puy, publisher of the *Indianapolis Freeman,* an abolitionist newspaper. According to the *Bugle,* some of Indianapolis's "first citizens" were involved in the incident, for a city councilman attacked De Puy. The publisher escaped, and the "mob made diligent search for him, for an hour afterwards." The next week some citizens, among them the Reverend Henry Beecher, either due to shame or recognition of the use that abolitionists might make of the murder, raised funds to hire two lawyers to prosecute the arrested man.[6]

Two other early black Indianapolis residents are found in Carter G. Woodson's *Free Negro Heads of Families in the United States in 1830.* Woodson also names Harry Perry and Samuel Brown as black heads of house in Indianapolis. His accounting, however, does not provide any information about the composition of those households. John Nowland, in *Early Reminiscences of Indianapolis,* tells us that Sam Brown came to Indianapolis from Kentucky with his son Willis and other family members in 1828. Brown and his family settled in the same neighborhood as the Gallatine and McKinley families, already established black residents of Indianapolis. Neither Gallatine nor McKinley appear as heads of separate households in the 1830 census, although both do so in later censuses.[7]

In 1840 it is more difficult to identify the members of black Indianapolis families. The manuscript census recorded 195 blacks living in the city that year. Except in one instance, blacks are checked off at the top of each tally sheet, as though the census taker simply stuck blacks at the top of whatever page he was working on.[8]

Furthermore, other sources indicate the continued separate residences of Sam Brown, Cheney Lively, Sampson Leatherman, and James Overall. Samuel Brown's will indicates that he owned forty acres of land and a house in Indianapolis. He appears again in the 1860 census as the head of house, and more than likely was also a resident in 1840. In 1834 Sampson Leatherman married Dinnah Allen in Indianapolis, and in 1835 he drew up a will leaving all real estate and personal property to her. James Overall's wife, Eliza, appears in the 1850 census as a propertied head of house. Perhaps James had died or simply was not in residence at that time, but the odds that the family had moved from the house he owned in 1840 are slim.[9]

Cheney Lively married John G. Britton in 1836, and they resided at her Maryland Street home. Britton, a black freedman who had migrated from Ohio in 1835, was a barber and became a leader in the black community. In January 1842 he participated in a meeting at Bethel AME Church in Indianapolis to plan a black state convention in Terre Haute the following May. Britton was the most active of the six Indianapolis men who organized that meeting. Blacks met in conventions throughout the antebellum period to consider practical ways to improve the condition of their race and to deal with the issues of African colonization, education, temperance, and racial/moral uplift. The Indianapolis meeting recognized the importance of blacks uniting in conventions and further resolved that "no colonization is a devoted friend to the moral elevation of people of color."[10]

Black Hoosiers strongly opposed African colonization. The 1849 Fort Wayne convention firmly rejected the notion that blacks would "enjoy civil and political privileges, and be truly independent in Liberia." Acknowledging that blacks were denied "the full enjoyment of liberty and pursuit of happiness . . . which are awarded to the whites," the convention reaffirmed blacks' determination "to use all lawful means, and to continue in so doing, until . . . allowed the full privileges of American citizens." Although some Indianapolis blacks emigrated to Canada after 1850 in response to Article 13 of Indiana's new constitution and the federal fugitive slave laws, very few of the city's blacks went to Liberia between 1849 and 1867.[11]

Those blacks who stayed in Indianapolis, like most antebellum blacks, saw education as a means of bettering their condition. An August 1847 city convention petitioned the legislature for "a reasonable share of the school fund . . . for the purpose of establishing schools among us, separate and apart . . . as we are prohibited on account of color, from sending our children to the district schools." Reporting that statewide blacks owned $249,980 in property, the convention pointed out to legislators that almost a quarter of a million dollars was taxed exclusively for the benefit of whites. The free school system in Indiana was not formally established until 1852, and, although blacks paid taxes, it was another seventeen years before the legislature changed the law to permit them to attend free public schools. In 1816 the first Indiana state legislature had passed a law providing education "equal for all," and some townships built schools. Race was not at issue in this law, so in the early 1800s some public schools accepted black students. By 1830, however, societal restraints did away with this practice. In 1843 the state legislature passed a school law prohibiting the attendance of black children in the same schools as whites.[12]

Black Hoosiers turned to private schools for education. Initially, even those schools refused blacks—although they were mostly Christian, church-run institutions. For a number of years

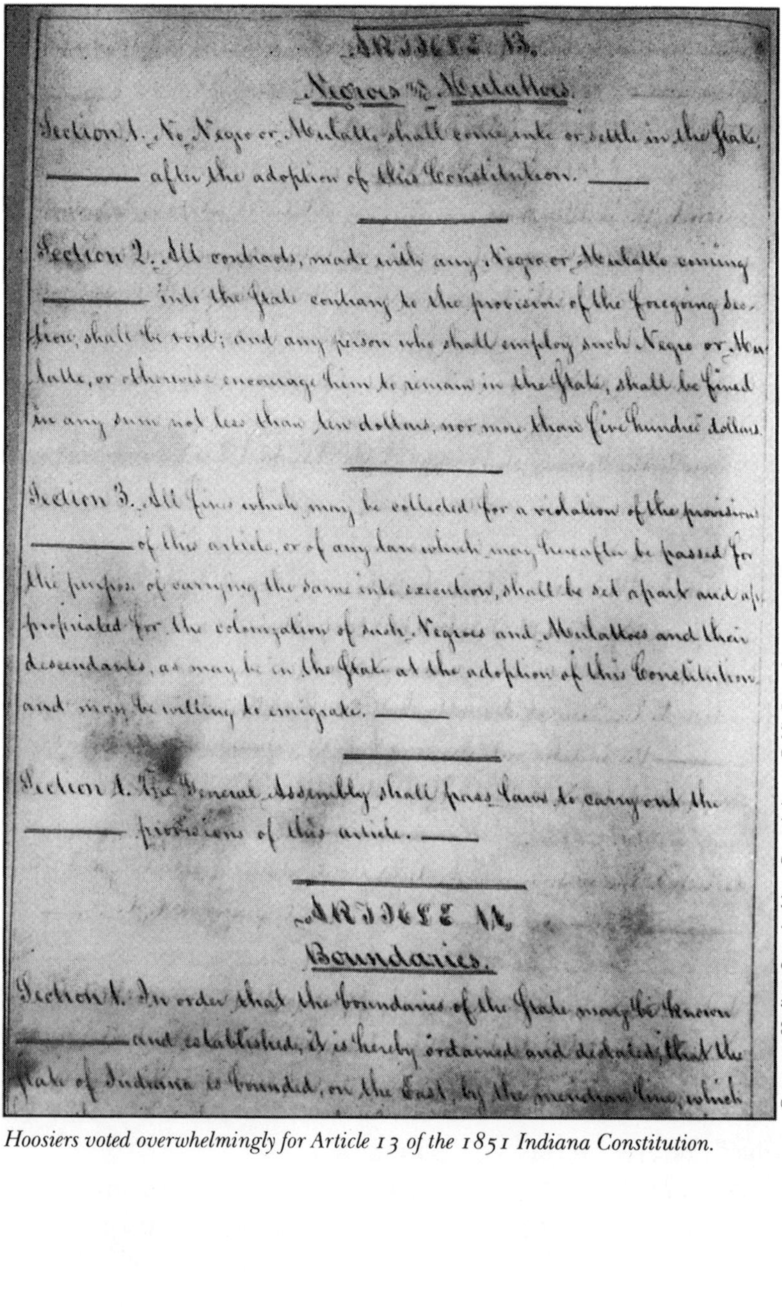

ARTICLE 13.

Negroes and Mulattoes.

Section 1. No Negro or Mulatto shall come into or settle in the State, after the adoption of this Constitution.

Section 2. All contracts, made with any Negro or Mulatto coming into the State contrary to the provision of the foregoing section, shall be void; and any person who shall employ such Negro or Mulatto, or otherwise encourage him to remain in the State, shall be fined in any sum not less than ten dollars, nor more than five hundred dollars.

Section 3. All fines which may be collected for a violation of the provisions of this article, or of any law which may hereafter be passed for the purpose of carrying the same into execution, shall be set apart and appropriated for the colonization of such Negroes and Mulattoes and their descendants, as may be in the State at the adoption of this Constitution and may be willing to emigrate.

Section 4. The General Assembly shall pass laws to carry out the provisions of this article.

ARTICLE 14.

Boundaries.

Section 1. In order that the boundaries of the State may be known and established, it is hereby ordained and declared, that the State of Indiana is bounded, on the East, by the meridian line, which

Courtesy of Indiana State Archives, Commission on Public Records

Hoosiers voted overwhelmingly for Article 13 of the 1851 Indiana Constitution.

Joseph J. Fitzgerald, pastor of Second Baptist Church in Indianapolis, gave private lessons to black students. In 1849, however, the Eleutherian College, a Baptist school in Lancaster, Indiana, opened its doors to black students. Another private school that antebellum black Hoosiers attended was Union Literary Institute in Randolph County. Samuel Smothers, who later became an AME minister in Indianapolis, attended Union Literary. He also served as the institute's principal for a time. Smothers was a successful businessman, who, at the time of his death, owned considerable real estate on Indiana Avenue, the hub of the black business community.[13]

The city's black population, however, also took the initiative to educate itself. Church Sunday schools taught students the rudiments of Bible reading. Black churches were also instrumental in the organization of schools. Bethel AME organized the first school for Indianapolis blacks. In 1858 Rev. Elisha Weaver served as its principal, and Lucy Jefferson assisted him. Geography, grammar, history, and physiology were offered in addition to the three Rs. In order to raise money for the school, Weaver and Jefferson staged exhibitions of their pupils' work. In 1859 Bethel AME organized an educational society to raise funds for the school. The black community was the school's main source of support through monthly dues and donations as well as tuition payments.[14]

It is not known just how many of Indianapolis's black children were able to attend school. In those days many children over the age of ten worked to help insure family survival. The 1840 census only reveals that forty-seven black children under the age of ten resided in twenty-four households—usually in family units. It is interesting to note that however difficult it must have been, blacks preferred to maintain their own separate residences. Few blacks were attached to white households as live-in servants.[15]

In 1850 Indianapolis blacks lived in 102 separate households. The census indicates that 21 percent of the 202 children (aged five to nineteen) in those households attended school. Sunday school tallies in that year indicate a class attendance of almost 28 percent of those young blacks. Fewer young Indianapolis boys attended school than girls, almost 25 percent less, probably due to the fact that more young boys tended to work outside the home at an early age. Blacks were attracted to urban areas by the employment opportunities that growing towns might offer and usually performed some sort of manual or domestic labor. The 1850 census indicates that twenty-five hundred blacks lived in Hoosier towns. Of those, 29 percent were laborers. Of the rest, 23 percent participated in sixty different skilled occupations, including blacksmiths, carpenters, brickmasons, plasterers, whitewashers, shoemakers, coopers, wagoners, and teamsters. The most frequently listed trade was that of barber. Antebellum barbers did more than just cut hair and give shaves. They provided many services to the community. Barbers acted as community doctors and dentists, dispensed news and information, and even provided banking services on occasion. Thus the barbershop was an important institution for the black community.[16]

Barbers were also members of other institutions that were central to the social life of the black community—fraternal organizations and churches. Indianapolis blacks formed sick and funeral benefit associations. In 1847 the Masons organized the first black lodge in Indianapolis, Union Lodge No. 1, under the auspices of the black Ohio Grand Lodge. The city's first Masonic lodge later united with Pythagoras Lodge to form Central Lodge No. 1. Gleaves Lodge No. 2 was organized in 1849. John G. Britton and James S. Hinton were the two most important Masonic leaders during the antebellum period, but it is not known where the Masons held their meetings.[17]

As was true elsewhere in the United States, separate black churches developed in Indiana denominations, and the Methodists were the most numerous. The first AME church in Indianapolis was Bethel AME. It was organized in 1836 and functioned as the only AME church in the city until 1866 when

In 1880 Republican James S. Hinton, an important Mason leader during the antebellum period, became the first African-American to serve in the Indiana General Assembly.

Allen Chapel began serving the community. Numerous benevolent societies and self-improvement groups were connected with Bethel AME Church. Bethel sponsored several literary and temperance societies as well as the Paul Quinn Missionary Society. The Baptist denomination had the second largest number of black Hoosiers. At least five black Baptist churches were organized in Indiana between 1831 and 1846. The "pioneer" black Baptist church in Indianapolis was Second Baptist. Organized in 1846 by the Reverend Charles Sachel, a missionary from Cincinnati, services were held initially in the home of Deacon John Brown. In 1849 the congregation built a little chapel on Missouri Street near the canal. The canal was used for baptisms, which were the focus of community celebrations until increased city population and sanitation problems made "sprinkling" a more desirable practice.[18]

The effectiveness of Indiana's exclusion policy, reinforced by the new state constitution adopted in 1851, is evident in census figures for the period. The growth rate of Indianapolis's black population decreased significantly at the end of the antebellum period. At the same time the white population increased by 130 percent. In fact, from the beginning to the end of the 1850s the total black population for the entire state increased from only 11,262 to 11,428; in Indianapolis from 405 to 498 in 117 households. This abatement of the steady increase in Indianapolis's black population during the 1850s was undoubtedly the result of several factors: the antiblack attitude of Hoosiers; the agitation for and inclusion of Article 13 in the 1851 Indiana Constitution, which excluded blacks from entering the state; the unavailability of jobs for blacks due to racism; and white Hoosier support for the fugitive slave laws. The blacks who resided in the state during the 1850s responded to those pressures in a convention held in 1851. John Britton, the convention's president, addressed the imminent adoption of Article 13 and the disfranchisement of blacks. Insisting that black Hoosiers were entitled to their full rights of citizenship, he nonetheless deplored the situation and urged blacks to consider possible emigration to Jamaica. Unfortunately, it is not known how many of Indianapolis's black citizens responded to this speech and actually left the city for Jamaica.[19]

While speakers at a gathering encouraged blacks to escape racist conditions by leaving the United States, others reaffirmed their native land. Recognizing that their condition was related to that of thousands of Americans who migrated from rural settings to crowded urban areas, some speakers proposed a different solution. Each year Indianapolis blacks celebrated 1 August as the anniversary of the emancipation of West Indian slaves with parades, speechmaking, and picnics. In 1851, one speaker at an Emancipation Day celebration encouraged blacks to leave the city, "where they were compelled to be the servants of white men," and move to rural areas where they might acquire real estate and live independently. He saw that their problems were not only the result of racism, but also of the rapid urbanization of the period. Racism, however, exacerbated intolerable urban conditions.[20]

The dramatic changes in urban environments of the 1850s and 1860s made those decades atypical of the antebellum period. Across the country, urban, foreign-born populations impacted negatively on two factors necessary to black community survival—housing and employment. The availability of another source of cheap labor further facilitated occupational discrimination against blacks, and the competition for housing, combined with the development of multifamily dwellings, aided in the segregation of blacks into tighter residential concentrations. Additionally, the Civil War added to those population pressures in Indianapolis. In the 1850s, due to restrictive legislation and fugitive slave laws, the city's black population increased only slightly. One of the impacts of the war, however, was to cause black refugees from the South to go north, so that by 1870 the black population of Indianapolis increased to 2,931 or 6 percent of the total city population of 48,244. The increase in the percentage of the aggregate was to have future consequences for Indianapolis blacks in terms of housing, education, and opportunity.[21]

Notes

1. Several texts are available about blacks in northern cities during the antebellum period. See Leon F. Litwack, *North of Slavery: The Negro in the Free States, 1790–1860* (Chicago/London: University of Chicago Press, 1961), and Leonard P. Curry, *The Free Black in Urban America, 1800–1850: The Shadow of the Dream* (Chicago: University of Chicago Press, 1981).

2. An account of black Hoosiers' legal status in the antebellum years can be found in Emma Lou Thornbrough, *The Negro in Indiana before 1900: A Study of a Minority*, vol. 37 of *Indiana Historical Collections* (Indianapolis: Indiana Historical Bureau, 1957), 1–31, 55–73, 99–129. Also see Paul Finkelman, "Slavery and the Northwest Ordinance: A Study in Ambiguity," *Journal of the Early Republic* 6 (Winter 1986): 343–70.

3. Jacob P. Dunn, *Greater Indianapolis: The History, the Industries, the Institutions, and the People of a City of Homes*, 2 vols. (Chicago: Lewis Publishing Co., 1910), 1:39; Edward A. Leary, *Indianapolis: The Story of a City* (Indianapolis/New York: Bobbs-Merrill Co., 1971), 8, 13, 47, 50; John H. B. Nowland, *Early Reminiscences of Indianapolis, with Short Biographical Sketches of Its Early Citizens, and a Few of the Prominent Business Men of the Present Day* (Indianapolis: Sentinel Book and Job Printing House, 1870), 95, 109; Thornbrough, *The Negro in Indiana*, 52.

4. *Population Schedules of the Fifth Census of the United States—1830.*

5. W. R. Holloway, *Indianapolis: A Historical and Statistical Sketch of the Railroad City* (Indianapolis: Indianapolis Journal Print., 1870), 80; B. R. Sulgrove, *History of Indianapolis and Marion County, Indiana* (Philadelphia: L. H. Everts & Co., 1884), 90; *Ohio Anti-Slavery Bugle*, 22 Aug. 1845; Thornbrough, *The Negro in Indiana*, 129–30.

6. *Indiana State Sentinel* (semiweekly), 19 July 1845; *Ohio Anti-Slavery Bugle*, 22 Aug. 1845; Curry, *The Free Black in Urban America*, Chapter 6.

7. Carter G. Woodson, *Free Negro Heads of Families in the United States in 1830* (Washington, D.C.: The Association for the Study of Negro Life and History, 1925); Nowland, *Early Reminiscences of Indianapolis.*

8. *Population Schedules of the Sixth Census of the United States—1840.*

9. DAR, *First Wills of Marion County*, 5 vols. (Genealogy Division, Indiana State Library), 1:64, 2:30; WPA *Index to Marriage Records, Marion County* (Genealogy Division, Indiana State Library), vol. 9, *1822–1850 and 1851–1855; Population Schedules of the Sixth, Seventh, and Eighth Censuses of the United States—1840, 1850, 1860.*

10. For an account of the black convention movement in Indiana see Howard Holman Bell, *A Survey of the Negro Convention Movement, 1830–1861* (New York: Arno Press, 1969); Thornbrough, *The Negro in Indiana*, 52.

11. For the proceedings of two of the Indiana conventions see Philip S. Foner and George E. Walker, eds., *Proceedings of the Black State Conventions, 1840–1865*, 2 vols. (Philadelphia: Temple University Press, 1979–80), 1:171–77; *The Non-Slaveholder* 3 (1848): 88; *Ohio Anti-Slavery Bugle*, 17 July 1849; Gwen Crenshaw, "The Apples of Sodom: The Colonization Movement in Indiana" (Unpublished paper, Indiana University, 1986); and *Indianapolis Freeman*, 23 Nov. 1844.

12. *Indianapolis Freeman,* 23 Nov. 1844.

13. *The Non-Slaveholder,* 88; Herbert Lynn Heller, "Negro Education in Indiana from 1816–1869" (Ph.D. diss., Indiana University, 1951); Thornbrough, *The Negro in Indiana,* 173–80.

14. Lori B. Jacobi, "More than a Church: The Educational Role of the African Methodist Episcopal Church in Indiana, 1844–1861," *Black History News & Notes* (Feb. 1988): 4–8; Holloway, *Indianapolis,* 238; Thornbrough, *The Negro in Indiana,* 151–56, 170–72.

15. *Population Schedules of the Sixth Census of the United States—1840.*

16. *The Locomotive,* 21 Dec. 1850; 14 June 1851; *Population Schedules of the Seventh Census of the United States—1850.*

17. See William H. Grimshaw, *Official History of Freemasonry among the Colored People in North America* (1903; reprint, New York: Negro Universities, 1969); Monroe N. Work, "Secret Societies as Factors in the Social and Early Economic Life of the Negro," in *Democracy in Earnest: Southern Sociological Congress, 1916–1918,* ed. James E. McCulloch, (Washington, D.C.: Southern Sociological Congress, 1918), 342–43; Dunn, *Greater Indianapolis, 1:* 278, 381–82; Thornbrough, *The Negro in Indiana,* 147–48.

18. For the early organization of black educational clubs and literary societies see Dorothy B. Porter, "The Organized Educational Activities of Negro Literary Societies, 1828–1846," *Journal of Negro Education* 5 (Oct. 1936): 555–76; Jacobi, "More than a Church," 4–8; Holloway, *Indianapolis,* 238, 219–20; Moses Broyles, *The History of the Second Baptist Church of Indianapolis* (Indianapolis: Printing and Publishing House Print, 1876); Thornbrough, *The Negro in Indiana,* 151–58, 170–72.

19. *Population Schedules of the Seventh and Eighth Censuses of the United States—1850, 1860;* Foner and Walker, *Proceedings of Black State Conventions,* 1:177.

20. *Indiana State Sentinel,* 3 July 1851; Holloway, *Indianapolis,* 114–15.

21. Curry, *The Free Black in Urban America,* xvi–xvii; Dunn, *Greater Indianapolis, 1:* 275–76; *Population Schedules of the Seventh and Eighth Censuses of the United States—1850, 1860.*

Biographies

Lillian Thomas Fox: Indianapolis Journalist and Community Leader

Earline Rae Ferguson

The scarcity of written records and sources makes the writing of black history difficult enough, but when one attempts to write a history of black women the difficulties are quickly multiplied, particularly for pre–World War I times. Not only are written records of black women's activities scarce to nonexistent, but also those histories and news reports that are available, whether written by men or women, seldom focus on or adequately mention black women.[1]

Late-nineteenth- and early-twentieth-century white Indianapolis newspapers, such as the *Star* and the *News,* noted infrequently the activities of the black community. If mentioned at all, individual blacks, usually males, were singled out when they were arrested in riots or police raids for gambling, or had allegedly attacked a white woman. They rarely were credited for contributions to the community, unless it was in an election year. At election time, when white candidates were interested in acquiring black votes, prominent black men were noted as supporters of this or that candidate. Black women, as nonvoters, were ignored.

The black Indianapolis press also seldom recognized Indianapolis black women. Black Indianapolis newspapers, such as the *Recorder,* the *Freeman,* and the *Colored World,* often published articles about and pictures of prominent black women in other parts of the country but seldom acknowledged Indianapolis women's activities. Basically, black Indianapolis newspapers only mentioned black women in their society columns, which were bulletin board–type listings of activities and meetings of various individuals, clubs, and church groups. One black woman, however, whom the black Indianapolis press did acknowledge was Lillian Thomas Fox, noted Indianapolis elocutionist, journalist, and clubwoman. Not only was she the subject of articles published in black newspapers, but also, more importantly, she was instrumental in the acquisition of white press coverage for black Hoosier men and women, particularly in the *Indianapolis News.*

Born in Chicago in 1866, Lillian Thomas came to Indianapolis in the early 1880s from Oshkosh, Wisconsin, where she spent her early childhood. She was the daughter of Rev. Byrd Parker, pastor of Quinn AME Chapel in Chicago. Her mother, Jane Janette Thomas, was one of the first black teachers in the Indianapolis public school system.[2] George Knox, the *Freeman*'s publisher, states in a posthumously published autobiography that Lillian Thomas came to Indianapolis in the early 1880s.[3] However, the first listing in the Indianapolis city directory for Lillian M. and Jane J. Thomas does not appear until 1886. Except for two years, the two women lived together until the mother's death at a house on West Street, which Lillian had renovated during the summer of 1884.[4] She also had an older brother about whom little is known. Lillian's younger brother, Charles T. Thomas, also lived in Indianapolis. Thomas's mother and brother died of tuberculosis within two days of each other in January 1894.[5]

Like most middle-class, nineteenth-century black women, Lillian Thomas did many different kinds of work in order to survive. At some point, probably prior to moving to Indianapolis,

Lillian Thomas Fox, 1866–1917

she was a stenographer for Garnet Transfer Company in Louisville, Kentucky.[6] After she came to Indianapolis, the 1888 city directory shows that she worked as a seamstress at her residence on Indiana Avenue. She began writing at a young age, but apparently took in sewing to meet her expenses. The *Freeman,* a nationally prominent black newspaper, observed that while her writing career may "not have been consecutive," it began when she was a young girl, before she came to Indianapolis.[7] However, it was after she moved to Indianapolis and studied with Madame Hattie Prunk, at the Indiana-Boston School of Elocution and the Indianapolis Institute for Young Ladies, that she refined her skills in dramatic reading and dialect and gained national prominence as a speaker.[8]

Thomas also used her writing talents in nonjournalistic positions in order to earn a living. In May 1891 she was one of the first Indianapolis blacks to take the civil service exam for clerkship. She made it clear, however, that her new endeavor would not interfere with her elocution studies and speaking engagements.[9] In September of that same year, Thomas accepted the position of assistant correspondence editor at the *Freeman*. She apparently had written for other newspapers, because the *Freeman,* in announcing her appointment to that post, remarked that "journalistic work is not new to the lady, she already having had considerable experience in that line." The *Freeman,* however, thought of her as a "professional elocutionist." In the same article the paper announced that "[i]t is not [Thomas's] intention to abandon her [speaking] profession, and [she] will from time to time fill engagements."[10]

Lillian Thomas achieved national recognition as a journalist through her work on the *Freeman*. Both white and black presses acclaimed her writing and reasoning abilities. At the same time, they also praised her speaking talents. During the early 1890s she made several "professional" tours of the Midwest and the South. Representative comments from these tours include praise for Thomas as "a lady of commendable ability and an enthusiastic friend of all that tends to lift up and improve the race" and "a very versatile and graceful speaker."[11]

At some point in her early travels Thomas met James E. Fox, originally from Jamaica in the West Indies. It is not known when Fox emigrated to the United States, but by 1893 he had become a prosperous merchant tailor in Pensacola, Florida.[12] At the end of May 1893, in keeping with the prevailing belief in the Cult of True Womanhood and the notion that a married woman's true sphere of influence was the home and the family, Thomas resigned from the *Freeman*.[13] On 25 May she married James Fox in a "modest" evening ceremony at her home on West Street, witnessed only by her mother, brother, and Rev. E. A. Williams, the pastor from Ninth Presbyterian Church who performed the ceremony.[14] Fox relocated his business to Indianapolis, opening a shop on Indiana Avenue opposite Odd Fellows Hall.[15]

While Lillian Fox curtailed her formal work commitment when she married James, she continued her involvement in church and elocution activities. She was an active member of Bethel AME Church[16] and attended AME state conventions.[17] She also participated frequently as both a speaker and an organizer in programs at other churches in the black community—at Jones Tabernacle, Simpson Chapel, Ninth Presbyterian, and Second Baptist, to name a few.[18]

Fox's speaking talents were also put to use in the early years of the black women's club movement. In December 1895 she accepted an invitation to speak at the Atlanta Congress of Colored Women.[19] The call for black women to meet in Atlanta was issued by the Ladies Auxiliary to the Cotton States and National Exposition, which was held in that city earlier in the year. At the congress she shared the speaker's podium with other notable black women activists such as Fannie Barrier Williams, Frances E. W. Harper, Victorian Earle Matthews, Lucy Laney, Dr. Lucy E. Moten, and Mrs. Booker T. Washington. Black women from twenty-five states and Washington, D.C., responded to the call and resolved to continue the formation of women's and children's clubs as part of their work for the "advancement of social purity, home improvement, and child culture."[20]

This was a resolution that Lillian Thomas Fox took seriously for the rest of her life. Already an active member of black Indianapolis literary societies, in 1903 she founded the Woman's Improvement Club (WIC) of Indianapolis[21] and East Chicago.[22]

In 1904 Fox sent out the statewide call for black clubwomen to meet at Bethel AME Church to form the Indiana State Federation of Colored Women's Clubs. She was president of the pro-tem organizing body and an honorary president of the federation until she died.[23]

On a trip from Indianapolis to the Atlanta Congress in 1895, Fox personally experienced the harshness of the Jim Crow laws. She had purchased a first-class ticket from Indianapolis to Atlanta on the Big Four route. Her first-class coach ride between Indianapolis and Cincinnati, where she had a one night layover, and the next day through the states of Kentucky and Tennessee was uneventful—until she reached Chattanooga. The conductor, who took charge of the train at that point, ordered her to leave the first-class coach and go to the section of the smoking car that had a partitioned compartment for blacks. Fox refused to move, and a heated exchange took place in which the conductor threatened to forcibly remove her either to the baggage car or off the train. Fox responded with assurances that any course of action that physically removed her from her seat "would prove the most expensive service [the conductor] had ever rendered the company by which he was employed." At that point the conductor stopped the train and threw off her satchel and lunchbox. Fox got off to collect her belongings and the train pulled away, leaving her in the middle of nowhere at 12:50 in the morning. Fortunately several passengers demanded that the conductor stop the train, and she was allowed back on but forced to sit in the back section.[24] Fox's experience on the Big Four was not an unusual one for black women who traveled—nor was her response. Like Ida B. Wells-Barnett and her case against the Chesapeake and Ohio Railroad in 1884,[25] Fox engaged counsel in Indianapolis and Atlanta and filed suit against the Southern Railroad. Unfortunately, unlike Wells-Barnett's successful suit, the outcome of Fox's case is not known. Like Wells-Barnett, however, Fox's experience did not discourage her from future travel; she continued to tour as an elocutionist and to attend church conferences.

Although Fox's continued attendance at national congresses of women's clubs has not yet been documented, more than likely she attended biennial meetings of the National Association of Colored Women's Clubs (NACW). The NACW was formed in 1896 to consolidate the several existing congresses of black women's clubs into one lasting national union.[26] In 1910 she accepted the NACW's invitation to address its members. Representatives from every state attended the NACW's Sixth Biennial Convention, held at the Methodist Episcopal Church in Louisville, Kentucky. Fox again shared the speaker's rostrum with other prominent black women activists such as Ida B. Wells-Barnett, who had compiled and published statistics about lynchings over a ten-year period.[27] Also addressing the convention were Nannie Burroughs, prominent black educator, and Elizabeth Ross, national secretary of the Colored Young Women's Christian Association.[28]

The *Freeman* does not mention whether Fox returned to work for that newspaper after her husband's death in 1898, but in 1900 Lillian Thomas Fox accepted a position as correspondent for the *Indianapolis News*.[29] Her Saturday column relating activities of the black community was the first to be published regularly in a white Indianapolis newspaper.[30] In addition to a regular column entitled "Notes [News or Accounts] of Colored People [Folks]," which listed the upcoming meetings and events of various organizations, Fox also wrote articles featuring local black men and women and news from national black conventions and gatherings, which usually appeared on the same page as the "Notes" column.[31]

The *News* never allowed Fox to write under a byline, but black newspapers make it quite clear that the *News*'s columns written about blacks were hers. She wrote in a graceful style that was at the same time simple, direct, and identifiable. The *News* distinguished infrequent articles it published about blacks from her work by use of the byline "The Staff of the *News*" and placement of the articles on a page other than the one on which the "Notes" column appeared.

Although the *News* did not formally acknowledge that Lillian Fox wrote the "Notes" column, she continued to do so for fourteen years, until ill health and failing eyesight forced her to take a leave of absence. When she left the *News* in 1914, she was the first black reporter to receive an indefinite leave of absence with pay. Fox passed on authorship of the column to Frances Berry, a black Indianapolis schoolteacher and fellow clubwoman. By that time, however, Fox had managed to increase the space allotted for her column and articles to approximately three-fourths of a page. She had also paved the way for other blacks to write similar columns at other white Indianapolis newspapers.[32]

Lillian Fox was ill for the last three years of her life, and the illness apparently curtailed her speaking and club activities.[33] The *Ledger* and the *Colored World*, both black newspapers oriented to "local news" more than the *Freeman*, do not indicate her participation in any speaking engagements or activities. In addition to failing eyesight, she had heart disease, and at the end of August 1917 suffered a stroke. She died on West 25th Street at the home of a friend, Florence Wayne, on 29 August 1917.[34] The Woman's Improvement Club and the Indiana State Federation of Colored Women's Clubs collected money to place a marker on her grave in Crown Hill Cemetery. This marker is located in the northwestern corner of the older section of Crown Hill. The marker reads "LILLIAN T. FOX, FROM INDIANA STATE FEDERATION OF COLORED WOMEN'S CLUBS." No dates of birth or death are included on the stone.

While it is not known where or even if she attended college, it is evident in all that one reads about her that Fox was an educated, "cultured" woman. None of the biographical articles that the *Freeman* published about Fox mentions that she had any college education. The *Freeman* particularly valued the educa-

IHS C2194

The Woman's Improvement Club operated the Oak Hill Convalescent Tuberculosis Camp in the Brightwood area of Indianapolis from 1905 to 1916. The camp was situated on a hill surrounded by large oak trees.

tion of blacks and was quick to credit them for any college or professional training. It is unlikely that if that newspaper had any knowledge of Fox's college education it would have omitted that information from the many articles that it published about her. Yet the *Freeman* was one of Fox's greatest admirers, characterizing her as "an original thinker and one who dare[d] to flout the dogma or philosophy be it ever so popular which do not consist with [her] cardinal principles of justice and right."[35] It was her concern with what was "just and right" that sustained her many political and welfare activities in the black Indianapolis community.

Those qualities that the *Freeman* attributed to Lillian Thomas Fox certainly facilitated her contacts with the white community and her hiring by the *News*. She clearly used those contacts and her position on the *News* to further the agendas of various groups within the black community and to highlight the activities of many previously obscure Indianapolis blacks. Among those groups that greatly benefited from the exposure she gave them was the Woman's Improvement Club, an organization that was to play a key role in the acquisition of health care facilities for black Indianapolis tuberculosis patients.

Notes

1. Standard Indianapolis histories that cover the late nineteenth and early twentieth centuries, such as Jacob Piatt Dunn, *Greater Indianapolis: The History, the Industries, the Institutions, and the People of a City of Homes*, 2 vols. (Chicago: Lewis Publishing Co., 1910); Clifton J. Phillips, *Indiana in Transition: The Emergence of an Industrial Commonwealth, 1880–1920* (Indianapolis: Indiana Historical Bureau and Indiana Historical Society, 1968); and Frederick Doyle Kershner, "A Social and Cultural History of Indianapolis, 1860–1914" (Ph.D. diss., University of Wisconsin, 1950), barely mention blacks at all—let alone black women. Even Ida Webb Bryant, who was herself a prominent black Indianapolis clubwoman and community leader, focused primarily on black men in her history of the black Indianapolis community, *Glimpses of the Negro in Indianapolis, 1863–1963* (Indianapolis: n.p., 1963).

2. Lillian Thomas Fox obituary, *Indianapolis News*, 29 Aug. 1917. Fox's death certificate lists Byrd Parker as her father and her mother as "unknown." Fox's obituary (which probably used the death certificate as a source) also names Byrd Parker as her father. Jane Janette Thomas's obituary (*Indianapolis Freeman*, 27 Jan. 1894) states that she was Lillian Thomas Fox's mother and the "relict" of Byrd Parker. It is unclear whether "relict" means that Jane Thomas was married to Byrd Parker or if she was Lillian Thomas's natural mother or stepmother. The 1888 Indianapolis city directory lists Jane Janette Thomas as the widow of Robert G. Thomas, so possibly Robert Thomas was her second husband and Lillian "Parker" used her stepfather's name.

3. George L. Knox, *Slave and Freeman: The Autobiography of George L. Knox*, ed. Willard B. Gatewood, Jr. (Lexington: University Press of Kentucky, 1979), 227 n. 68.

4. *Indianapolis Freeman*, 18 Aug. 1888.

5. Ibid., 27 Jan. 1894; Marion County Board of Health, death certificates for Jane Janette Thomas and Charles T. Thomas.

6. John William Gibson and William Henry Crogman, *The Colored American from Slavery to Honorable Citizenship* (Atlanta: Hertel, Jenkins and Co., 1905), 196. In 1892 the *Indianapolis Colored World* remarked that Lillian Thomas returned "home" to Louisville, Kentucky, for a visit, so it is probable that she lived there before she came to Indianapolis. *Indianapolis Colored World*, 10 Sept. 1892.

7. *Indianapolis Freeman*, 22 Dec. 1894.

8. Ibid., 2 May 1891.

9. Ibid.

10. Ibid., 9 Jan. 1892.

11. Ibid., 13 June, 22 Aug. 1891.

12. Knox, *Slave and Freeman*, 227 n. 68; *Indianapolis Freeman*, 3 June 1893.

13. For the relationship of black women to the doctrine of the Cult of True Womanhood, see Tullia Brown Hamilton, "The National Association of Colored Women, 1896–1920" (Ph.D. diss., Emory University, 1978).

14. *Indianapolis Freeman*, 3 June 1893.

15. Advertisements for Fox's shop frequently appeared in ibid. beginning 12 Aug. 1893.

16. In 1892 Fox was organizing vice president of the Bethel AME Church's Christian Endeavor Society. Ibid., 18 June 1892.

17. Ibid., 20 and 29 June 1896.

18. Ibid., 20 Jan., 11, 18 May 1895.

19. Ibid., 21 Dec. 1895. This issue contained a notice of her invitation to address the Atlanta Congress. Fox also wrote a series of articles about the congress, two of which appeared in the *Freeman* on 25 Jan. and 1 Feb. 1896. The concluding articles in that series were not published. The *Freeman* became involved in an antilynching campaign, and the subsequent issues were devoted to covering those activities. Fox herself was one of the organizing members of the Indianapolis Anti-Lynching League and spoke at the 1894 organizational meeting. Ibid., 8 Sept. 1894.

20. Charles Harris Wesley, *The History of the National Association of Colored Women's Clubs: A Legacy of Service* (Washington, D.C.: National Association of Colored Women's Clubs, Inc., 1984), 35. Other sources placing late-nineteenth- and early-twentieth-century black women in a historical framework include: Sharon Harley and Rosalyn Terborg-Penn, eds., *The Afro-American Woman: Struggles and Images* (Port Washington, N.Y.: Kennikat Press, 1978); Bert James Loewenberg and Ruth Bogin, eds., *Black Women in Nineteenth-Century American Life: Their Words, Their Thoughts, Their Feelings* (University Park: Pennsylvania State University Press, 1976); Paula Giddings, *When and Where I Enter: The Impact of Black Women on Race and Sex in America* (New York: William Morrow and Co., Inc., 1984). Information on most of the women who spoke at the 1895 Atlanta Congress can be found in Darlene Clark Hine, *When the Truth Is Told: A History of Black Women's Culture and Community in Indiana, 1875–1950* (Indianapolis: National Council of Negro Women, Indianapolis Section, 1981), 38.

21. Hine, *When the Truth Is Told*, 38.

22. Wesley, *History of the National Association of Colored Women's Clubs*, 446.

23. *Souvenir Booklet Containing Historical Sketches of Indiana Federation of Colored Women's Clubs up to and Including Twenty-First Annual Convention at Gary, August, 1924*, p. 5; Wesley, *History of the National Association of Colored Women's Clubs*, 434–35.

24. *Indianapolis Freeman*, 11 Jan. 1896.

25. Giddings, *When and Where I Enter*, 22–23.

26. See Hamilton, "National Association of Colored Women," for a thorough account of the formation of the NACW.

27. Ida B. Wells-Barnett's daughter, Alfreda M. Duster, has edited her mother's diary, *Crusade for Justice: The Autobiography of Ida B. Wells* (Chicago/London: University of Chicago Press, 1972). It contains a complete and personal account of her activities in the era of the Jim Crow laws.

28. Wesley, *History of the National Association of Colored Women's Clubs*, 69.

29. *Indianapolis Ledger*, 7 Feb. 1914; *Indianapolis Recorder*, 7 Feb. 1914; *Indianapolis News*, 29 Aug. 1917; 19 Feb. 1940.

30. *Indianapolis Ledger*, 7 Feb. 1914. My own examination of the *Indianapolis Star* and *Indianapolis News* in the 1890s has found no earlier regularly published column on the black community.

31. These articles were published in line with the "Notes" column, as though they were the lead-in to it. The subjects of these articles coincided with the events black newspapers indicate that Fox was instrumental in publicizing—i.e., the Pythian convocations of the early 1900s. *Indianapolis Ledger,* 7 Feb. 1914.

32. By the time of Fox's death, the *Indianapolis Daily Times* regularly published a column on Saturdays about the black community, focusing primarily on church groups. The format for that column was remarkably similar to Fox's "Notes" column. This is possibly the column that Mrs. Ruth Clinthorne remembers that her father, Rev. Henry Herod of Second Christian Church, wrote for a white newspaper in the early 1900s.

33. Woman's Improvement Club (WIC) Manuscript Collection, Indiana Historical Society, Indianapolis, Indiana. The 1916–18 ledger shows that Fox was less active in that club's meetings during that period. It mentions a note that Fox sent the WIC ladies expressing her regret at being unable to meet with them and her hope to be well enough soon to be with them again.

34. Marion County Board of Health, death certificate for Lillian Thomas Fox; *Indianapolis News,* 29 Aug. 1917.

35. *Indianapolis Freeman,* 22 Dec. 1894.

Buster Hall—Hoosier Hero of the Ninety-Ninth Squadron

Arville L. Funk

On 2 July 1943 a flight of United States B-25 bombers was completing its bombing runs on the enemy airfield at Castelvetrano, Sicily, when suddenly a pair of German Focke-Wulfs (FW-190) dropped in behind the last two bombers and moved in for the easy kill. Out of nowhere, a P-40 Warhawk, with the name "Maxine/Knobly II" emblazoned on its nose, dived between the last bomber and the two FW-190s, and within seconds the last FW-190 trailed black smoke and headed for the ground. The German plane crashed, raising a cloud of dust.

This victory by the escorting P-40 from the Ninety-ninth Squadron would become a historic moment in aviation history, as it was the first occasion when a black pilot of the United States Army Air Corps shot down an enemy plane.[1] The honor of this victory went to 1st Lt. Charles Blakely "Buster" Hall, a twenty-two-year-old from Brazil, Indiana.[2] Actually, the first black American to destroy an enemy plane in combat was Eugene Jacques Bullard, who flew with the French Air Force in World War I. Bullard had tried to enlist in the United States Army Air

Charles B. Hall

Corps in 1917, but had been denied entry, officially because of flat feet.[3]

Charles Hall, the son of Frank and Anna Hall, had been an outstanding athlete at Brazil High School. He participated in football, basketball, and track, and when he graduated in the spring of 1938 the nation was still recovering from the depression.[4] He wanted to attend college and discovered that his athletic ability was his key to a college education. He enrolled at Eastern Illinois University at Charleston in the fall of 1938 and played halfback on the football team during his first two years at the university.[5]

During the spring quarter, 1941, Hall withdrew from college to enlist in the United States Army Air Corps. He hoped to be accepted in the aviation cadet training program. After completing basic training, Hall was assigned to Class 42F at Tuskegee Institute. After much pressure from several black leaders, the

Army Air Corps photograph

This photograph, taken in March 1943 at the Tuskegee Army Air Field, includes the original pilots of the Ninety-ninth Pursuit Squadron. (Front row, l. to r.:) Herbert E. Carter, Amory, Mississippi; Lee Rayford, Washington, D.C.; George S. Roberts, Fairmount, West Virginia; Benjamin O. Davis, Jr., Washington, D.C.; Lemuel R. Curtis, Hartford, Connecticut; Clarence C. Jamison, Cleveland, Ohio; Charles B. Hall, Brazil, Indiana. (Middle row, l. to r.:) Walter I. Lawson, Newton, Virginia; Spann Watson, Hackensack, New Jersey; Allen G. Lane, Demopolis, Alabama; Paul G. Mitchell, Washington, D.C.; Leon C. Roberts, Pritchard, Alabama; John W. Rogers, Chicago, Illinois; Louis R. Purnell, Germantown, Pennsylvania; James T. Wiley, Pittsburgh, Pennsylvania; Graham Smith, Ahoshie, North Carolina. (Back row, l. to r.:) Willie Ashley, Jr., Sumter, South Carolina; Charles W. Dryden, New York City; Irwin B. Lawrence, Cleveland, Ohio; William A. Campbell, Tuskegee, Alabama; Willie H. Fuller, Tarboro, North Carolina; Richard C. Davis, La Grange, Georgia; Sidney P. Brooks, Cleveland, Ohio; Sherman W. White, Montgomery, Alabama; George R. Boling, Phoebus, Virginia. Not pictured are Sam M. Bruce, Seattle, Washington; Herbert V. Clark, Pine Bluff, Arkansas; James B. Knighten, Tulsa, Oklahoma; and James L. McCullin, St. Louis, Missouri.

United States government consented to accept blacks into aviation cadet training. The Ninety-ninth Pursuit Squadron was activated in January 1941 to receive the first black pilots to complete flight training.[6]

Hall was assigned to civilian flight instructor James T. Wiley at Tuskegee.[7] Flight training at Tuskegee Army Air Field was accomplished in three phases: primary, basic, and advanced. During the middle of Hall's training, Wiley joined the Air Corps and finished advanced training with Class 42F. Charles Hall and the other members of Class 42F graduated and were commissioned second lieutenants in July 1942.[8] Hall was well liked by his fellow cadets, and he was often referred to as "Sea-Buster" or "Buster."[9] Class 42F was the fourth class of pilots to graduate from Tuskegee, and the graduates from all four classes were assigned to the Ninety-ninth Squadron, commanded by Lt. Col. Benjamin O. Davis. They flew P-40 Warhawks.[10] Hall was not the first Hoosier pilot to graduate from the Tuskegee Army Air Field. Lt. Charles H. DeBow from Indianapolis had been a member of the first class of aviation cadets (Class 42C) who graduated on 6 March 1942. DeBow later retired from the Air Force as a lieutenant colonel, after serving as commanding officer of the 301st Fighter Squadron in Italy.[11]

On 15 April 1943 the Ninety-ninth Squadron, which included twenty-eight pilots, left Camp Shanks, New York, and boarded the SS *Mariposa* sailing for the North African Theater.[12] On 24 April the *Mariposa* reached Casablanca, French Morocco, in North Africa, and after disembarking, the Ninety-ninth airmen were assigned to the Thirty-third Fighter Group and received new P-40s.[13]

On 31 May the Ninety-ninth, still under the command of Davis, arrived at Farjouna, Cape Bon, just south of Tunis, to train to fly combat missions with the Twelfth Air Force. Finally on 2 June the Ninety-ninth flew its first combat mission.[14] Lieutenants William A. Campbell, Clarence C. Jamison, James T. Wiley, and Charles "Buster" Hall were selected to fly the historic mis-

Charles DeBow (right) was a member of the first class of the Tuskegee Army Air Field graduates.

sion.[15] The four black pilots flew as wingmen with four white pilots from the Thirty-third group. Their mission was to bomb the Italian island of Pantelleria, and each of the P-40s carried a single five hundred-pound bomb. After completing the first successful mission, the group flew a second mission the same day. No enemy aircraft were encountered, and all planes returned safely without any damage. One week later six pilots of the Ninety-ninth were engaged with enemy fighters while on a mission, and although no German planes were shot down, this marked the first occasion when black United States Army Air Corps pilots engaged enemy planes in aerial combat.

After the surrender of Pantelleria, the Ninety-ninth Squadron moved to El Haouria, Tunisia, and was assigned to the 324th Fighter Group under the command of Col. Leonard C. Lydon.[16] The Ninety-ninth was given the duty of escorting medium bombers to the western sector of Sicily. On 2 July six P-40s from the Ninety-ninth were on that historic mission when Lieutenant Hall shot down the FW-190. Hall's own account was as follows: "It was my eighth mission, but the first time I had seen the enemy close enough to shoot at. I saw two FW-190s following the Mitchells just after the bombs were dropped. I headed for the space between the fighters and bombers and managed to turn inside the jerries. I fired a long burst and saw my tracers penetrate the second aircraft. He was turning to the left, but suddenly fell off and headed straight into the ground. I followed him down and saw the crash. He raised a big cloud of dust."[17]

Lieutenant Hall received much attention from the press for his feat and was personally congratulated by Gen. Dwight D. Eisenhower after the mission.[18] The black newspapers in the United States especially brought the news of Hall's victory to the American public.

Buster Hall was to fly many more missions with the Ninety-ninth Squadron during the next several months, serving as Flight C Commander.[19] Capt. George "Spanky" Roberts, the operation officer and later commanding officer of the Ninety-ninth Squadron, was impressed with Hall's conduct in battle, and he described Hall as "totally without fear."[20] On 28 January 1944 Hall, who had become a captain, and members of his patrol group over Italy intercepted seven German fighters that were beginning their strafing run on allied positions at Anzio. The Ninety-ninth patrol dove into the middle of the German formation, and Hall shot down a Messerschmitt (ME-109) and a FW-190. In his report Hall described his actions, "I intercepted a Messerschmitt flying on the deck, very low. I gave a couple bursts (the P-40 was armed with six 50-calibre machine guns) and saw it crash and burn. I turned over and saw the Focke-Wulf and gave it three bursts. It did the same thing."

For this feat Hall was awarded the Distinguished Flying Cross by General Eisenhower. On that same mission, another Hoosier pilot, Lt. Wilson Vashon Eagleson, Jr., also downed an enemy plane.[21] Eagleson was a member of a prominent family in Bloomington. His great-grandfather, H. V. Eagleson, was born in St. Louis, but migrated to Indiana after the Civil War. Initially, the family moved to a small black community near Chambersburg in Orange County. They later moved to Mitchell in Lawrence County and then to Bloomington. Eagleson's three sons, William, Walter, and Preston, served in the military: William in the Spanish-American War and Walter and Preston in World War I.[22]

The son and grandson of Wilson Vashon Eagleson, Sr., and Preston Eagleson, respectively, Lieutenant Eagleson entered Indiana University in fall 1940. Like Buster Hall, he left college in 1941 and enlisted in the Army Air Corps.[23] After his training at Tuskegee, he joined the Ninety-ninth Squadron and flew with Hall on many missions over North Africa and Italy. Eagleson also shot down an enemy plane in February 1944.[24]

After completing eighty-seven missions, Captain Hall returned to the United States in 1944. With five others from the Ninety-ninth, he went on a bond-selling tour for the war effort, appearing and speaking at bond rallies in several cities.[25]

The Ninety-ninth Squadron served gallantly in the Italian Theater until May 1945, earning twelve campaign battle stars and three distinguished unit citations. The Ninety-ninth was followed by other black squadrons in Europe. These later squadrons included several Hoosier pilots, including Lt. Earl Burton Highbaugh from Indianapolis. Lieutenant Highbaugh flew a P-51 fighter plane in combat in Europe. He was killed in January 1945 while on a mission.[26]

When Maj. Charles Hall was discharged in 1946, he relocated to Oklahoma City and worked at Tinker Field. Later he joined the Federal Aviation Agency (FAA), where he was employed at the time of his death on 23 November 1971.[27] Hall stated his feelings for his country in a letter that he wrote home in 1943. His simple expression spoke for many of his comrades in the Ninety-ninth Squadron.

"Up in the blue it doesn't make any difference where you come from, what color you are, etc. I can appreciate the land, sea, engineers, cooks, nurses, Red Cross, tanks, defense workers, people buying bonds and a thousand and one other things. I look at them and say: 'This is worth fighting for.' Over here (Italy) one learns to appreciate the small things, the things that used to seem unimportant. I've seen a lot of men go down on both sides. We get to know each other like brothers. It hurts us but we must carry on, and we will. I've been very lucky; I know that it is through prayer and luck that I have made it so far. I realize more every day that there is unity through strength. Pray for us all."[28]

NOTES

1. Robert A. Rose, *Lonely Eagles: The Story of America's Black Air Force in World War II* (Los Angeles: Tuskegee Airmen, Inc., 1976), 58.
2. William P. Schlitz, "From Tuskegee to Space," *Air Force Magazine* (Feb. 1983): 77.
3. James W. Burke, "The Black Eagle," *The Retired Officer Magazine* (May 1984): 30.
4. *Brazil Times*, 9 Sept. 1985.
5. Luther C. Hicks, *Great Black Hoosier Americans* (Indianapolis: Luther C. Hicks, 1977), 32.
6. John Hope Franklin, *From Slavery to Freedom: A History of Negro Americans* (New York: Vintage Books, 1969), 584.
7. Letter to author from James T. Wiley, 4 Nov. 1985.
8. Letter to author from Herbert E. Carter, 21 Oct. 1985.
9. Mitch Mitchell, "99th Fighter Squadron at War," *Air Classics Magazine* (Feb. 1987): 16.
10. Edward C. Gleed, "The Story of America's Black Air Force," *Tony Brown's Journal* (Jan./Mar. 1983): 6.
11. *Lonely Eagles Calendar*, Tuskegee Airmen, Inc., 1985, p. 11.
12. Letter to author from William Campbell, 21 Oct. 1985.
13. Ibid.
14. Schlitz, "From Tuskegee to Space," 77.
15. Letter to author from William Campbell, 21 Oct. 1985.
16. Rose, *Lonely Eagles*, 58.

17. Ibid.

18. *Pittsburgh Courier,* 10 July 1943.

19. Letter to author from James T. Wiley, 4 Nov. 1985.

20. Rose, *Lonely Eagles,* 58.

21. Frances V. Halsell Gilliam, *A Time to Speak: A Brief History of the Afro-Americans of Bloomington, Indiana, 1865–1965* (Bloomington: Pinus Strobus Press, 1985), 45.

22. Forest M. Hall, *Historic Treasures* (Bloomington: Indiana University Press, 1922), 110, 156.

23. Gilliam, *A Time to Speak,* 45.

24. Rose, *Lonely Eagles,* 64.

25. *Norfolk Dispatch,* 15 Dec. 1944.

26. *Indianapolis News,* 10 Jan. 1945.

27. *Brazil Times,* 9 Sept. 1985.

28. Ibid.

H. J. Lewis and His Family in Indiana and Beyond, 1889–1990s

Marvin D. Jeter

H. J. Lewis has been called "the first black political cartoonist" on the basis of his work for the Indianapolis Freeman *from 1889 to his untimely death in 1891. But, no collection of his illustrations in this genre has ever been published, and his full life story has not been outlined until recently.*

My associates and I have recently worked on a multimedia project, including exhibits,[1] television programs,[2] and a book,[3] commemorating Lewis's life and works. Here, I will only briefly summarize his life before he moved to Indiana in 1889 and his work for the Freeman. *I will concentrate instead on selected aspects of his life in Indiana and will also note some relevant aspects of the lives of his descendants.*

This essay is a distillation from, and an outgrowth of, two "working papers" published in Black History News & Notes.[4] *Those papers called attention to several gaps in our information about Lewis, and they also contained some conjectures that turned out to be mistaken. When the first paper was written, I had not yet heard the tape of a 1968 interview with Lewis's son Chester Arthur Lewis.[5] In the second, I expressed some hope of finding at least one living descendant or relative of H. J. Lewis and have since been amply rewarded by a number of conversations and communications with his granddaughter Anna*

Lavinia Lewis, of Cambria Heights, New York. Thus some of the gaps have been filled, and most if not all of the errors corrected.

Henry Jackson Lewis was born into slavery in Water Valley, north-central Mississippi, probably in 1837. Essentially nothing is known of his early childhood, except for the fact that during infancy he fell into a fire, crippling his left hand, disfiguring the left side of his face, and blinding his left eye.[6] He never went to school but taught himself to read and write, and was also apparently largely self-taught as an artist.[7]

Lewis's whereabouts before, during, and after the Civil War years are unknown, but by 1872 he had bought a lot near downtown Pine Bluff, Arkansas, and must have built a house there shortly afterward. Also about that time he married Lavinia Dixon, who was born some time between 1845 (according to the Chester Lewis interview) and 1855 (according to the 1880 census).[8]

The Lewises had seven children, all born in Pine Bluff. Their first child, John W. Lewis, was born about 1875. The other children were Richard Augustus, ca. 1877; Lillian Estella, ca. 1879; Elizabeth Victoria (the Lewises appear to have been very "Victorian" Americans in their aspirations), ca. 1881; Chester Arthur on 19 January 1883 (Chester A. Arthur was then president); Henry W., ca. 1885; and Frances Louise, ca. 1887.

H. J. Lewis was listed in the 1876–77 Pine Bluff city directory as a laborer, and he stated later that he had "learned something about the carpenter's trade," so he must have worked only part-time as an artist at first. But by 1879 he had sold several drawings of Arkansas Valley scenes in and near Pine Bluff to *Harper's Weekly*, which had them redone by staff engravers for publication. Similarly, in 1882 he sold some drawings of Mississippi Valley flood scenes to *Harper's*. Later that year, the *Pine Bluff Commercial* referred to him as a promising "caricaturist and pencil artist." Shortly thereafter he began a brief stint working with

While working with Dr. Edward Palmer in 1882, Lewis produced this drawing of a mound located at Walnut Lake Station near Dumas, Desha County, Arkansas.

Dr. Edward Palmer of the Smithsonian Institution, drawing Indian mounds in Arkansas and adjacent states.[9]

With the possible exception of a pencil portrait of Thomas Dansby, a white friend from Pine Bluff, there are no Lewis drawings that date from mid-1883 through 1888. Also, there are virtually no statements about his activities during these "lost years." However, we do have his own 1889 statement that "only four years ago" he ran out of work in Pine Bluff and went to Little Rock (about forty miles up the Arkansas Valley, to the northwest), where he was hired as a porter for the *Arkansas Gazette.* He added that while there he watched some white engravers at work and learned some of their techniques.[10]

In January 1889, at the age of about fifty-one, Lewis moved from Pine Bluff to Indianapolis and joined the staff of the *Freeman,* which had been reorganized by Edward E. Cooper in July

1888. Cooper participated significantly in the "black bolt" from the Republican party at that time and supported the incumbent Democratic president, Grover Cleveland, in the

THE NATIONAL EXECUTIVE ASLEEP.

Indianapolis Freeman, 19 October 1889

November election. However, Indiana Republican Benjamin Harrison won. By the end of the year Cooper was converting the *Freeman* from a rather staid format to a lively illustrated one, billed as "a National Illustrated Colored Newspaper" and "the *Harper's Weekly* of the Colored Race," and was preparing for some vigorous attacks on the Harrison administration.

H. J. Lewis's cartoons were among the major weapons in these attacks. One example shows President Harrison "Cooling the Ardor" of a black aspirant for an ambassadorship. Harrison is surreptitiously helped by Secretary of State James G. Blaine. Another example shows "The National Executive [Harrison] Asleep" but about to be awakened by two black men sounding the alarm with bugles. Numerous other Lewis cartoons reiterated similar political and racial themes.

Lewis was joined by his wife and family in Indianapolis in early 1889. His self-portrait, published in the *Freeman*'s 13 July 1889 issue, shows a boy and girl behind his likeness. A ribbon attached to the boy's hat bears the initials "J. W. L.," and one fluttering from the girl's neck has the initials "L. E. L." These refer to Lewis's oldest son John W. Lewis, and his oldest daughter Lillian Estella Lewis. In the background are the Brooklyn Bridge and the Eiffel Tower, engineering marvels that had just been completed.

Another Lewis drawing was used as a heading for the "Our Women" column in a number of late 1890 and early 1891 issues of the *Freeman*. The original is in the Burroughs Collection at the Du Sable Museum of African-American History in Chicago and bears a handwritten label identifying it as a portrait of his wife Lavinia Dixon Lewis. According to Chester Arthur Lewis, our only source of information about her, she had no formal education, but "did a great deal to help Father with thoughts and ideals." Also, she "was considered a prominent elocutionist in Indianapolis. . . . [We children] had another example, the excellent mental expression of this remarkable woman—my mother."[11]

Indianapolis Freeman, 13 July 1889

H. J. Lewis self-portrait

Chester Arthur Lewis's recollections of his father are somewhat scattered throughout the interview. After initially referring to him as "perhaps one of the nation's leading cartoonists," he added:

> Father was more than a cartoonist, he was an artist in almost every aspect of significant art, or historical art. He could draw, he could carve wood—in fact, he made his [wood] plates for reproduction in the newspaper. He was an all-around man. His drawings were the capstone of his work.
>
> Father was perhaps a most unique, and definitely a highly critical person, with reference to race relationships,

which at that time were . . . kind of [awry?]. That is to say, the Negro had no particular recognized status in the country at the time; it was left entirely to the Negro[es] to establish themselves, and they had begun. Father had become a leader in attempting to portray the value of the Negro as an American, and to inspire the Negro, and to help the people of the nation to realize that the Negro and the whites were here together, and let the Negro have a right and . . . exercise that right to the best of [his] ability, to establish the fact that he was a good American citizen and a good American.

In the beginning there were wonderful [white] people who were free of the bias of slavery . . . but he had difficulty finding [enough?] people who could understand. He had a very difficult time, and this was the thing that prompted him to attempt to do something about it, with his drawings, and with the effort to establish, through the publication of the *Freeman,* the fact that the Negro was here, and was responsible for himself, and was determined to establish himself as [an] American citizen. It was Father's desire, as the artist and cartoonist, to portray the full opportunity of the benefits that lay in the minds and hearts of the people, to fully express themselves as responsible citizens of the community.

Father was . . . sort of a wizard. He seemed to have known almost all there was to know at that time. . . . This, I learned later, was the salvation of people, any people—white people, black people—to know the facts, [to] know the truths relative to themselves and their opportunity to participate in the program of helping to establish the democratic nation that we have a right to boast about.[12]

During the interview Lewis commented on only one of his father's drawings that he donated to the Du Sable Museum. This was one entitled "[Colored?] Americans Making Their Mark," showing a variety of black people stretching to make their highest possible marks on a blackboard. It has not been found in any of the existent copies of the *Freeman,* nor in any other publication. Like the rest of the original drawings in this collection, it

Courtesy of the Du Sable Museum of African-American History

"[Colored?] Americans Making Their Mark"

was probably made during the last year or so of H. J. Lewis's life; it may never have been sold to a publisher. Whether or not it was ever published, his son offered these comments on its intended message:

> This was, perhaps, one of the great cartoons, so far as the Negro people [are] concerned, demonstrating to them that they were free to develop and exercise the opportunity to develop themselves. . . . Father was attempting to pinpoint, for their benefit, the responsibility that rested on them to fit into the nation; . . . working to sustain themselves and contribute to the growth and progress and prosperity of the nation.[13]

Lewis apparently produced only a few drawings of Indianapolis scenes. This is unfortunate because he was quite skilled as an architectural artist. One interesting example is his 1889 sketch of the proposed Indiana [Civil War] Soldiers and Sailors

Monument. At that time the cornerstone had just been laid in a ceremony attended by five thousand people including President Harrison. The monument was not completed until 1902 and is now perhaps the most famous landmark in Indianapolis.

One of Lewis's few locally oriented political cartoons shows "the grand rush [of job applicants] for Mr. [William] Wallace's office after his nomination [by Harrison] for Post-master at Indianapolis" in early 1889. Above the building's entrance is a sign reading "Ingall's Block," and one of the windows is labeled "The Model."

A final example, from the Du Sable Museum's collection, shows a streetcar labeled "Irvington Citizens' Street R. R." rolling through an almost rural landscape. Irvington was an eastern suburb of Indianapolis. The drawing was published as a humorous cartoon in the *Freeman*'s 23 August 1890 issue, with "Mrs. Fromthesouth" asking an elderly man, "What kind of folks are these Yankees, anyway? They came down south and freed the poor colored folks, and now . . . they have come north and freed the mules!"

The black population of Indianapolis had grown from only 498 in 1860 to 2,931 in 1870; 6,504 in 1880; and 9,133 in 1890.[14] This last figure would have included the Lewises. Their first place of residence was on South Olive Street. Chester Arthur Lewis recalled the address as "in the eleven hundred block," but the 1890 city directory listed Henry J. Lewis as living at 321 South Olive Street and his occupation as an engraver. This location is on the southeastern outskirts of the downtown section, less than a mile from the *Freeman*'s offices on Pennsylvania Street.

The son also remembered moving "quite a distance" to a house on Lincoln Lane, where they were living when his father died in 1891. This address was given as 34 Lincoln Lane in one of his obituaries and in the 1891 Indianapolis city directory, which listed H. J. Lewis as an artist. The house was located in the northwestern suburbs across the White River. The move probably reflects a brief period of prosperity for the Lewis family.

Lewis's occupational status was a rare one among Indiana blacks of this period. A study made after the 1890 census showed that only 2,287 black men out of the total population of more than 45,000 were in skilled trades. By far the largest skilled class was barbers, with 699 members. Also, there were 185 miners or quarrymen; 162 iron and steel workers; 154 railroad engineers or firemen; 133 carpenters; 130 brickmakers; only 15 machinists; and 14 printers. The numbers of professionals such as doctors and lawyers were very small, in the single figures during this period.[15]

H. J. Lewis died 9 April 1891. In a brief obituary notice, the *Indianapolis News* stated, "He was never well in this severe climate, and died of pneumonia." He was buried in an unmarked grave at the Mount Jackson Cemetery, on the western outskirts of downtown Indianapolis.

His widow was left with the six younger children at home. She moved with them to a house on Shelby Street, about a half block from Fountain Square and fairly close to their former home on South Olive Street. Quite probably, this near-downtown location would have provided more job opportunities for the family.

There was also a strong spiritual element that held the family together through these difficult times and undoubtedly influenced at least two of the sons' choices of careers. As summarized by Chester Arthur Lewis:

> At the Christmastime, it was purely spiritual, and we were taught of the humility of the Christ, and the manifestation of His preaching and teaching, as it comes to us, to so live that we reflect credit upon ourselves rather than attracting animosities of those around, with whom we live and dwell. This calls for something that perhaps we did not fully recognize, and it pertained to a fulfilling of the right to make contributions, the right to give as well as seek ourselves, in

> spite of the fact that all we had was our willingness to work, and to find work that would compensate us to the extent of meeting our responsibility as fellow citizens.[16]

The oldest son, John W. Lewis, had moved out on his own, but at first found only sporadic work available. The widow had to take on domestic work—washing, ironing, and cooking—to support her children. She maintained a strict discipline and "did not permit us to take liberties with learning, or anything else . . . we used to get pennies, and nickels, and dimes, for expressing our thoughts on things of the nation."[17]

Lavinia Dixon Lewis was still very much the head of the family in 1903 when Chester Arthur Lewis, then twenty years old, obtained her permission to leave for St. Louis. Anna Lewis remembers her grandmother in the 1920s and 1930s as "a very lovely woman" who was "very devout and spent much of her time in religious activities."

The Lewis family was thoroughly imbued with the "work ethic" and the desire to become as fully integrated as possible into the American version of late-Victorian society. There were some difficulties in adjusting to public schooling, but the home environment was remarkably supportive of self-education, as described by Chester Arthur Lewis:

> Most of the children . . . could be said to be self-educated, and this is not unusual at this period. . . . We knew pretty well much of the literature of the community, publications and things of that kind . . . my brother [John] saw to it that we had the periodicals that appeared in those days. . . . [We] had a peculiar situation of the children prodding each other, and attaining a definite knowledge of what was going on, what was taking place, and of course we were inspired by Mother.
>
> We were like gadflies. We would sting each other into an excellent expression of the thing that confronted us, and wouldn't accept anything short of [a] factual expression of what was brought before [us] in the papers, and publications, and so forth.[18]

John W. Lewis, the oldest son, was characterized by Chester Arthur as follows:

> My brother John did not have the advantage of schooling, because his temperament would not allow him to begin as a beginner. He followed after Father's footsteps, became an artist, and traveled extensively [elsewhere he is said to have had "a mind of his own" and to have been "in the Pullman service for quite a while"], and finally he was the first of the family to marry, and establish his own home. He settled in Indianapolis.[19]

He worked for the *Freeman* as a teenager, apparently as a sort of "printer's devil." (One of H. J. Lewis's drawings, ca. 1890, shows a teenager, probably John W. Lewis, running errands in the *Freeman*'s composing room.) Later, he worked mainly for other newspapers, generally as a cartoonist and artist, and in other capacities. By 1916 he was listed as "manager" for the *Indianapolis Colored World.* (Ironically, his father and Cooper had been engaged in a bitter "newspaper war" with the *Colored World* in 1889–91.) He also worked briefly for another black paper, the *Indianapolis Recorder.* He had no children, died in 1919, and was buried at Crown Hill Cemetery on the northern outskirts of downtown Indianapolis, as were most of his siblings and his mother Lavinia Dixon Lewis.

The next oldest son (and child), Richard Augustus Lewis, "reached the seventh or eighth grade in school," according to Chester Arthur Lewis, who added,

> He worked in the community at most any available job, until he finally found an acceptable position with the John Koch furniture store . . . and was sufficiently employed there, and he married. . . . [He] held that job for years, in fact until he passed on.[20]

He married, was widowed, married again, and had seven children with his second wife Lillie Ann Wale Lewis. She was born at West Point, Kentucky (near Fort Knox) and attended Kentucky State University. Three of their children and one granddaughter are still living. According to his daughter Anna Lavinia Lewis he also had artistic talents, as did all of his siblings. He could draw, paint, carve, and did calligraphy. He died in 1963 at age eighty-five and is buried at Crown Hill.

Chester Arthur Lewis did not discuss his sisters' educations and later lives in the taped interview, except to note that the youngest sibling, Frances Louise, had died about the age of thirteen. According to Anna Lavinia Lewis, two sisters, Lillian Estella Lewis and Elizabeth (Isabel or Belle) Lewis, never married. Elizabeth was particularly talented artistically. Both of them lived and died in Indianapolis and are buried at Crown Hill Cemetery.

Chester Arthur Lewis spoke humorously of his own early years:

> I might say that my schooling was quite nil. I was sufficiently impetuous with reference to schooling [that I] didn't understand the teachers, the teachers didn't understand me, and I ran away from home. I got my education partially from extension universities, like the LaSalle Institute, and there was also an International [Correspondence] School, and then extensive reading, because my oldest brother had accumulated quite a library, and I loved reading, and just got busy and I got sufficient learning to get along pretty well for myself anywhere and everywhere.[21]

After going to St. Louis in 1903, he married and became a Baptist minister. He lived for some time in Chicago and was entrusted with about fifty of his father's drawings after his mother's death. In 1968 he donated the drawings to the Du Sable Museum of African-American History in Chicago. Dr. Margaret Burroughs, the museum's cofounder, and the late Eugene Feldman, one of the museum's earliest and most vigorous supporters, conducted the taped interview of the octogenarian. Chester Arthur Lewis died in Indianapolis in 1974 and is buried at Crown Hill Cemetery.

Henry W. Lewis was "perhaps the best-schooled of the family

and got lessons from the extension universities of the country," according to his brother. He was listed in city directories as a student, artist, and salesman in his early years, then became a successful real estate and insurance agent in the 1920s. He was very close to his mother, who lived in his home in later years, and often helped out at his office. Her staunch religious faith undoubtedly was a strong influence on him. By the 1930s he also went into the Baptist ministry, and after her death founded the Lavinia Dixon Lewis Memorial Tabernacle, serving as its pastor. (His brother remarked that he was "prominent in the ministerial circles of Indianapolis.") However, fire destroyed the church in late 1968; Henry W. caught pneumonia as a result and died in November of that year. He is buried at Crown Hill.

All of H. J. and Lavinia Dixon Lewis's grandchildren were born at home in Indianapolis to Richard Augustus Lewis and his second wife Lillie Ann Wale Lewis. They were Lillian Estella Lewis Woodward (1908–1943), Anna Lavinia Lewis (b. 1913), Byrdie Wale Lewis (b. 1914), Audrey Henrietta Lewis (1917–1963), Susie Virenda Lewis (1918–1978), Richard Augustus Lewis, Jr. (1922–1986), and Rose Hummons Lewis Taylor (b. 1924).

Anna Lavinia Lewis graduated from Purdue University, majoring in French and English, but found employment teaching science in New York City. Determined to continue her French studies, she took graduate courses at New York University, Hunter College, and Columbia University. She also excelled as a musician, playing the violin in an orchestra that performed in Carnegie Hall. She moved to France in 1948, attended the Sorbonne, and met eminent classical musicians such as Pablo Casals and Alexander Schneider. She returned to New York in 1958 and taught until her retirement in 1975. Since then she has lived in Cambria Heights, a suburb in the borough of Queens.

Byrdie Wale Lewis attended Howard University, where she majored in psychology, and worked in the United States civil service in Washington, D.C., until her retirement. She still lives in Washington.

Richard Augustus Lewis, Jr., worked in Indianapolis for the post office and the fire department, attaining the rank of captain. He had excellent artistic talents, especially as a woodworker, but became blind due to diabetic complications in his latter years. His widow, Maggie Lewis, still lives in Indianapolis.

Rose Hummons Lewis Taylor was named for Rose Elizabeth Dent Hummons, the first wife (d. 1946) of Dr. Henry L. Hummons, Sr. (1873–1956), a pioneer black physician and civic leader in Indianapolis during the first half of the twentieth century.[22] (Dr. Hummons was Lillie Wale Lewis's obstetrician for the births of all of her children, according to Anna Lewis.) Rose married George Taylor, a social worker like herself; they are now retired and living in Queens, New York. The Taylors have one daughter, Terri Rose Taylor—H. J. and Lavinia Dixon Lewis's only great-grandchild. Appropriately, she works in the publishing business in New York.

The productive and constructive lives of H. J. Lewis's descendants underscore the concluding comment made about him by E. E. Cooper in his obituary notice in the *Freeman* of 18 April 1891, wishing for Lewis "a completer life, where conditions may not interfere, or man's narrowness or unfair hatred prevent the full expression of his unique and striking gifts."

Notes

1. The exhibit "Black and White: The Art of H. J. Lewis" was prepared by the staff of the Old State House Museum in Little Rock, Arkansas, and opened there in February (Black History Month) 1991. It ran until July 1991, in the process commemorating the centennial of Lewis's death (April 1891 in Indianapolis). It included the surviving originals of pencil sketches of Arkansas Indian mounds borrowed from the Smithsonian Institution's National Anthropological Archives, combined for the first time with the surviving originals of his pen-and-ink drawings, loaned by the Du Sable Museum of African-American History in Chicago, plus photocopies of selected *Freeman* drawings. A photographic traveling version of the exhibit opened in September 1991 at the Jefferson County Historical Museum in Pine Bluff, Arkansas (where Lewis lived during most of his adult life), and ran through November. The traveling exhibit commemorated

Black History Month, 1992, at the State Historical Museum (Old State Capitol), in Jackson, Mississippi, the state in which Lewis was born.

2. "UAPB Outlook" program, moderated by Eva McGee, director of Broadcast Media Dept., University of Arkansas at Pine Bluff, and broadcast on KATV, Channel 7, Little Rock, on 23 February 1992. Also videotapes produced by La'Tonya Richardson of UAPB Broadcast Media, featuring the Lewis traveling exhibit at the Jefferson County Historical Museum, and the Arkansas Archeological Society/Survey 1991 "Summer Dig" at the Taylor Mounds site (which was drawn by Lewis in 1882).

3. Marvin D. Jeter, *H. J. Lewis:* Freeman *Artist* [in preparation].

4. Marvin D. Jeter, "Henry J. Lewis: A Researcher's Note," *Black History News & Notes* (Nov. 1989): 3, 7–8; "H. J. Lewis, *Freeman* Artist: A Working Paper," ibid. (Aug. 1990): 3–8.

5. Chester Arthur Lewis, 1968 taped interview by Dr. Margaret Burroughs of the Du Sable Museum of African-American History, Chicago.

6. The account of Lewis's accident is related in a brief article headlined "Relied on Himself," *Indianapolis Journal,* 24 Nov. 1889. The article contains the only known interview with direct (and indirect) quotations attributed to Lewis, and I am most grateful to Wilma Gibbs and her colleagues at the Indiana Historical Society for finding it.

7. Statements to this effect were published in an article about the Arkansas mound investigations in *Frank Leslie's Illustrated Newspaper,* a New York weekly, vol. 56, 26 May 1883, p. 222. Similar statements also were made in the 1889 *Indianapolis Journal* article and in the 1968 interview with Chester Arthur Lewis.

8. The 1880 Pine Bluff census gave the family name as "Dickson," but I am using the family's rendering of "Dixon" as given in their Indianapolis documents, including the "Lavinia Dixon Lewis Memorial Tabernacle" listing in the city directories of the 1960s.

9. All of the surviving Lewis drawings of Arkansas mounds have been published in Marvin D. Jeter, ed., *Edward Palmer's Arkansaw Mounds* (Fayetteville: University of Arkansas Press, 1990). His drawings of mounds in adjacent states have been published in a related article: Marvin D. Jeter, "The Palmer-Lewis 'Mound Survey' Forays into Tennessee, Mississippi, and Louisiana, 1881–1884," *Mississippi Archaeology* 25 (2): 1–37.

10. *Indianapolis Journal,* 24 Nov. 1889. The *Gazette,* long acclaimed as "the oldest continuously published newspaper west of the Mississippi," was founded in 1819 and survived until its regrettable demise in late 1991.

11. Chester Arthur Lewis, 1968 interview.

12. Ibid.

13. Ibid.

14. Emma Lou Thornbrough, *The Negro in Indiana before 1900: A Study of a Minority,* vol. 37 of *Indiana Historical Collections* (Indianapolis: Indiana Historical Bureau, 1957), 229.

15. Ibid., 349, 365–66.

16. Chester Arthur Lewis, 1968 interview.

17. Ibid.

18. Ibid.

19. Ibid.

20. Ibid.

21. Ibid.

22. "Henry L. Hummons Collection," *Black History News & Notes* (Nov. 1987): 1.

The Architecture of Samuel M. Plato

Katherine M. Jourdan

Samuel M. Plato, a prominent architect, spent the early years of his career in Indiana. He came to the Hoosier state in 1902, and, as a Marion resident, designed some of that town's finest churches, homes, and buildings.

Plato was born in Waugh, Montgomery County, Alabama, in 1882. His parents were James and Katie Hendricks Plato. The elder Plato was a farmer but also practiced carpentry among several other trades. He had been apprenticed to Samuel Carter, a noted black artisan, who bequeathed his tools to Plato after his death.[1] It has been suggested that Plato named his son Samuel after Carter, who was a close family friend. From his father, Samuel Plato learned many of the building skills that would serve him later in life.

As a youngster Plato attended Mount Meigs Institute, which was established near his home in Alabama. After graduation he studied an additional year in Winston-Salem, North Carolina. At this point Plato attempted to enter Tuskegee Institute, but apparently could not afford the tuition. He attended the State University in Louisville, Kentucky, which was later renamed Simmons University.[2] In 1898 Plato began a normal course at the State University, which he followed with college courses with the intention to study law.

Plato completed some small furniture projects during his childhood, and as a young adult he constructed a farmhouse on Bardstown Road outside Louisville for Dr. C. I. Purce, president of State University. He also constructed a commercial building

Marion Chronicle-Tribune Magazine, 9 July 1978

Samuel M. Plato, 1882–1957

that was part retail and part post office for a client named Grant. Grant influenced Plato to follow his aptitude toward building and to use his mechanical talent.[3] While attending the university, Plato learned of the International Correspondence School in Scranton, Pennsylvania. He received permission to add correspondence courses to his other studies and thereby acquired courses in architecture and carpentry through this method of study.

Following the completion of his education Plato moved to Marion, Indiana, where he rented a home at 431 North Boots Street. Plato may have chosen to move to Marion because of the city's growth that followed the discovery of gas in 1887. His move to the city in 1902 was at the end of the gas boom era. Initially, Plato found his search for jobs frustrating because the local building contractors would not hire him. He found jobs doing carpentry finishing, work which eventually led to building contract leads within the community. Although there is not a complete list of the buildings Plato designed while in Marion, he is credited as the architect for several projects.

One of Plato's early projects was the Second Baptist Church located at 1824 South Branston Street. The congregation is reported to have raised the money for the construction by selling meals and performing odd jobs. The simple Vernacular structure with wood siding was completed in 1905 and is graced by a number of stained-glass windows. The building was purchased in 1967 by the Full Gospel Church and is currently used as a house of worship. The structure, remodeled with aluminum siding, is in good condition.

It was probably during the early stage of his architectural career that Plato designed five or six cottages along Pennsylvania Avenue next to the railroad at 10th and Boots streets. These identical homes were in the Carpenter-Builder style and were probably used by the employees of the U.S. Glove Factory, located across the tracks. Today only one structure remains, and it is heavily damaged on one side due to a fire that demolished the home next to it. After these earlier works, Plato expanded his style sense and adopted popular elements and designs being expressed by other early-twentieth-century architects. These details included Classical Revival elements and Arts and Crafts motifs.

One Grant County history states that Plato constructed School No. 2 in Weaver.[4] This small, black, rural community developed at the crossroads of 600 S and 300 W in Marion during the nineteenth century. The school replaced a previous structure erected in 1869 after money was obtained from the Indiana legislature to build a school for blacks. The new brick structure was in the Romanesque Revival style and operated as an educational facility until 1945. The building had a rusticated limestone foundation and square corner tower with an arched doorway. The structure was similar in style to other schools remaining in Jay and Blackford counties from the same period. The building was documented with photographs and measured drawings for the Historic American Buildings Survey (HABS) before it was razed in 1977.

After his arrival in Marion, Plato formed a partnership with black building contractor Jasper Burden. His son, Everett Burden, described Plato in a 1978 *Marion Chronicle-Tribune Magazine* article as "a solemn, slow-talking man who dressed plainly and shunned publicity."[5] For nearly ten years Plato and Burden teamed together for a number of building projects in Marion.

Little is known about Plato's personal life. His first wife, Nettie, is buried in Marion. His second wife, Elnora Davis Lucas, was the daughter of George Davis of Alexandria, Indiana. She had attended several design schools and was operating an exclusive dressmaking business when she married Plato.[6]

Plato's name was given to an apartment complex that he designed at Adams and 15th streets in 1910. The Platonian Apartments, with their fine craftmanship and expensive interiors, became home for the elite society of Marion. The U-shaped complex is comprised of three buildings with ten two-story units. These buildings, with their Arts and Crafts details, are still in use today as rental property. Although briefly owned by Marion College (Indiana Wesleyan University), they are once again in private hands. At one time an underground heating plant located on the northeast corner of the lot heated the apartments. Today each unit has a basement with utilities. The first floor has a living room, a dining room, and a kitchen, and the second floor has two bedrooms.

As his work became well known in the community, a prominent Marion citizen, J. Woodrow Wilson, engaged Plato to design and build a home. Wilson and his friend, millionaire John Schaumleffel, encouraged Plato in his work and often supported his bond for various construction projects. The brick Neoclassical home is one of the finest structures in the city. Constructed in 1912 as a wedding present for Wilson's wife, Lillian Pampell, the fifteen-room house has a third-floor ballroom with a stage. Plato liberally used classical details with the

Courtesy of Katherine M. Jourdan

The Hostess House, Inc., also known as the Wilson-Vaughan House, is listed on the National Register of Historic Places.

home's front facade being dominated by a two-story, full-height porch supported by colossal fluted Ionic columns. The facade has a pedimented gable with a deep entablature. In the center of the gable is an oculus window that opens onto the ballroom stage. The first floor is rich in details, with molded plaster designs on the ceilings and repeated arch doorways with fanlights. The home was only occupied a few years before J. Woodrow Wilson's death in 1916. His widow later married Dr. John Colin Vaughan, and after the stock market crash the doctor took up a medical practice in Marion. The Vaughans died during the 1940s. The Hostess House, Inc., was formed in 1950 by a group of local women to purchase the home as a women's center; this group continues to use the home for its activities. The interior of the home was refurbished the same year. The Wilson-Vaughan home was listed on the National Register of Historic Places (NRHP) in 1988.

In 1913 Plato received a commission to design and build the First Baptist Church on the northwest corner of 4th and Nebraska in Marion. The site was unusual inasmuch as the church had to span Boots Creek, which crossed part of the lot. Plato again used many Classical Revival details in the design of the brick church. The basic plan was used on six other structures after Plato left Marion, including the Broadway Temple African Methodist Episcopal Zion Church (662 South 13th Street) and the James Lee Memorial Church (1754 Frankfort), both located in Louisville. These structures are listed on the National Register. The First Baptist Church was utilized until 1974, when the congregation built a larger facility across 4th Street. Until 1987 the building was owned by the city and used as a senior citizens center. By the end of 1988 a small church congregation owned the building and was holding services.

Plato was listed in the 1919 Marion city directory as living at 2309 South Boots. The Foursquare house was adjacent to an identical structure located at 2306 South Boots, and both structures are attributed to Plato. His office in 1919 was listed as

S206 Marion Block in Marion. This address was the Zimmerman Building, which housed the Queen City women's store on the first floor. The building was later razed and replaced by a parking lot.

Around 1920 Plato constructed a Mission-style bungalow at 722 South Washington Street for David Lavengood. Presumably there was some disagreement between Lavengood and Plato about the floor plan and details regarding the construction of the house. A year was spent reworking the interior of the house before it was accepted by the owner. Since 1945 George G. Richardson, a local dentist who uses it as a residence and office, has owned the structure. The brick house, with an attached garage and tile roof, has two entrances and is in excellent condition.

Plato left Marion sometime between 1919 and 1921 to return to Louisville. While in Louisville he continued his architectural work. He designed several buildings, including the aforementioned churches, two banks, the Virginia Avenue

Courtesy of Katherine M. Jourdan

Samuel M. Plato designed numerous churches, post offices, and houses, including First Baptist Church in Marion, Indiana.

School, and William H. Stewart Hall at Simmons University. A residential area that he helped construct was named Plato Terrace in his honor.

After 1940 Plato became involved with federal projects. He was one of the few blacks to be awarded defense housing and post office contracts. Plato is credited with designing and constructing over thirty-nine post offices across the nation. Some of the site locations include Frankfort, New York; Decatur, Alabama; Phillipsburg, New Jersey; Coatesville, Pennsylvania; New Philadelphia, Ohio; Morgantown, West Virginia; and Xenia, Ohio. Each building varied in design with a mixture of Classical or Gothic details.

One of Plato's largest governmental contracts was an 88-unit housing project constructed as part of a 250-unit complex of civilian housing at Curtiss Wright Defense Plant in Louisville. When the plant closed after World War II, it operated as a governmental public housing project. During the 1950s, with Fannie Mae financing, the Fincastle Heights Mutual Ownership Corporation was formed, and the complex was operated as a cooperative. It is currently known as Fincastle Apartments.[7]

Plato designed a 304-unit public housing complex in Sparrows Point, Maryland, near Baltimore. After World War II he built two government dormitories, Midway and Wake, in Washington, D.C.

In 1945 Plato continued to demonstrate his architectural versatility with the building of Westover in Louisville. As the contractor of this subdivision located on South Western Parkway opposite Chickasaw Park, Plato built two-bedroom houses. The houses, which were to be sold to black families, received financial support from the Mammoth Life Insurance Company.[8]

Plato died in Louisville in May 1957.[9] His buildings remain, however, as evidence of his talent as an architect. Several of his structures have achieved the recognition of being placed on the NRHP. Certainly there are many others deserving of this high honor of distinction. Since Plato worked not only on a local scale but also on a national level, many of his buildings have yet to be rediscovered by scholars. As long as man protects and cares for the built environment, Plato's piles of wood, brick, and stone will continue to contribute to our architectural heritage.

Notes

1. Amalia Ray, "Samuel Plato," *Negro History Bulletin* (Dec. 1946): 51.
2. Marion Porter, "Friends Helped Him Succeed, Negro Contractor Here Declares," *Louisville Courier-Journal,* 28 July 1941.
3. Ray, "Samuel Plato," 53.
4. Rolland Whitson, *Centennial History of Grant County, Indiana, 1812–1912,* 2 vols. (Chicago and New York: The Lewis Publishing Co., 1914), 1:354.
5. Jerry Miller, "People of Color: Grant County's Black Heritage," *Marion Chronicle-Tribune Magazine,* 9 July 1978.
6. Ray, "Samuel Plato," 71.
7. Ann S. Hassett to the author, 20 Apr. 1987, private papers.
8. Ed Edstrom, "Louisville's Next Two Years Hold Good and Bad, Developers Find," *Louisville Courier-Journal,* 16 Sept. 1945.
9. Obituary, "Contractor S. M. Plato Is Dead at 75," *Louisville Courier-Journal,* 15 May 1957.

William Edouard Scott: Indianapolis Painter

William E. Taylor

The long and tiring journey of John and Eliza A. Johnson Scott, grandparents of William Edouard Scott, came to an end in 1847. They had traveled by ox cart from Salem, North Carolina, to Indianapolis, and they eventually settled on the west side at 1124 Senate Avenue. Thus began the Scott era in the West. William's father, Edward Miles Scott, married Caroline Russell, and in 1882 they became the parents of a daughter. On 11 March 1884 a son was born.[1]

William E. Scott attended public school in Indianapolis, and although the regular elementary school studies held his interest art was his first love. After he completed elementary school, he enrolled in Manual Training High School. At Manual, Scott became the only black member of the track team.[2] While at the high school, he became known as one of the best students in drawing ever to attend the school. Otto Stark, chairman of the art department, took a special interest in Scott and advised him to seek enrollment at the Chicago Art Institute. After graduation Scott spent the summer of 1903 in Chicago. He achieved some artistic success by selling two portraits for five and fifteen dollars. Also, a wealthy black woman contracted him to draw the plans for a flat to be built in Chicago. At the end of the summer Scott returned to Indianapolis and took a job in the art department at Manual to earn enough money to enroll at the Chicago Art Institute. He assisted in the instruction of freshman drawing students and was in charge of the art supplies. A greater asset for Scott may have been the opportunity that he had to study drawing for another year under the guidance of Otto Stark. At nineteen years of age, Scott was planning to become a sculptor, and he looked forward to enrolling in architectural, life drawing, and sculpture classes at the Institute.[3] One cannot measure the influence of Otto Stark or how the sale of the portraits in Chicago may have persuaded Scott to consider painting and drawing as a major in school instead of sculpture.

By fall 1904, when Scott had saved sixty-five dollars, he took the money and his portfolio to the Chicago Art Institute to enroll in classes. Fortunately, some of his work was brought to the attention of John Vanderpoole, the teacher of the life drawing class. Although the nude life class represented work by third-year students, Scott was given a trial period in the class. He was successful. After paying for three months tuition and a registration fee, Scott had little left of his sixty-five dollars. He obtained a job sweeping the classrooms mornings and evenings to pay for his tuition. He had another job at a restaurant waiting tables at dinner, which paid fifty cents and a meal. Scott later said that the restaurant lost money on the meal since it was the only one that he could afford, so when he ate it was three meals rolled into one. He also cut hair, mended shoes, and did laundry, which enabled him to stay at the Institute his first year.[4] After that year, his drawing ability helped him win competitions with other students for illustration jobs with magazines. The magazines would send stories that the winning student would illustrate. Scott's drawings were featured in *Inland Printer, Outing, Redbook,* and *Voice* magazines.[5]

Scott attended classes at the Institute for five years. He won a number of prizes, a school scholarship, and honorable mentions. During his senior year he was awarded the prestigious

Frederick Magnus Brand first prize for pictorial composition. As a student, his proficiency as a mural painter did not go unnoticed. During his last year in school he did mural decorations for five public school buildings in Chicago, including the mural *Commerce* for Lane Technical High School. He also had works accepted in the public schools of Washington, D.C., and Evanston and Highland Park, Illinois.[6] When he graduated in June 1909, Scott left Indianapolis for France. He had planned to be gone for two years and divide his time between Paris, Holland, and Italy. When he arrived in France, the only French that he knew was "give me some bread, please" and "thank you." When he attempted to order a meal in a restaurant he would sometimes receive a strange array of food on his plate. As an artist he thought that it would be a good idea to take his drawing pad with him and draw a picture of what he wished to order. What may have seemed like a good idea to him, most of the time was left to the waiter's interpretation of his drawings. One time he showed a waiter a drawing of pork chops; the waiter served him a meal of mutton. After several months in Europe his money problems became critical. Henry O. Tanner, the major black artist in Europe, was in Paris at that time. Hearing about Scott's financial plight, Tanner invited him to stay at his summer home located in Trepied, an artist colony. He told Scott that he was welcome to the potatoes in the cellar. Later, Scott recalled, "Potatoes I cooked in every known and unknown way and my only variety was—potatoes."[7] From information gathered from various sources, records indicate that during this period Scott studied at the Julian Academy. However, what may have been more important was his opportunity to study with Tanner. Scott reflected upon the relationship: "Studying with Mr. Tanner was a source of great inspiration to me. He is painstakingly conscientious and a real genius."[8] Studying at the Julian Academy and under the tutelage of Tanner, along with very hard work by Scott, resulted in his having three paintings accepted at the Salon des Beaux Arts at Toquet.[9]

Courtesy of John W. Lee

William E. Scott, 1884–1964

After about fifteen months in Europe, Scott returned to the United States. He had only enough money to buy his passage to America and a train ticket to Chicago. When he arrived in Chicago he had a dime in his pocket.[10] He had relatives living in Chicago at that time, who may have provided him a place to stay.

The exhibition and sales of his artwork earned him enough money to return to Europe.[11]

In the spring of 1912 the great spring salon in Paris accepted Scott's painting, *La Pauvre Voisine*.[12] Tanner also had a painting at the salon; they were the only blacks in the show. For Scott, this was an achievement of great note. The French newspapers wrote about his artwork and reproduced the painting in the papers. The painting was also reproduced on postcards in full color. Publicity about the painting came to the attention of government officials of the Argentine Republic, and his painting was purchased for six hundred dollars. Later Scott recounted the sale of the painting:

> I sent a picture to the Salon, and on the advice of a friend, Balfour Ker, a great American illustrator, put a price of $1000 on it. He said, "Scott, you are not going to sell it anyway, so make the price big." At the opening of the Salon I had about $10 in excess of my passage home. I had prepared to return to America when I received a letter from representatives of the government of the Argentine Republic asking the lowest price I would accept for the picture. With as little money as I had I would have gratefully accepted $5, but, thinking the whole proposition a joke, I named a price of $600. Much to my surprise I received a check for that amount. I remained in France a year longer on that money.

With this success came another honor in 1913. The Royal Academy in London and the Salon at La Loque, France, accepted Scott's paintings.[13] He was now on his way to becoming a major figure in the art world on two continents.

Scott returned from Europe in the fall of 1912 with twenty-six paintings. They were put on exhibit at the Indianapolis Otto Stark Studio, located at 1722 North Delaware Street.[14] The exhibit was both an artistic and financial success. One of the paintings was an impressionist scene of a little French town during an evening rain. Etaples, located in Normandy, was one

Shortridge High School Collection, Indiana State Museum

La Miseré, *an oil painting on canvas, won the Tanguary prize at the summer salon of the Paris-Plage in 1913.*

of the places Scott had a studio, and it was also where Tanner had a studio in his semiretired years. In 1918 the "colored people of Indianapolis" purchased the painting, titled *Rainy Day Etaples,* and presented it to the Herron Art Institute for its collection.[15]

After painting three murals in Chicago, Scott was commissioned to paint murals in a few of the public schools in Indianapolis. The school administrators in the Indianapolis system were implementing a new concept called "the school beautiful." Since young people spent most of the year within the walls of a school building, the administrators felt the atmosphere needed to be bright and attractive. On two occasions an Indianapolis newspaper reviewed dedications of Scott's school murals. Dedication exercises were held on 7 February 1913 for a mural painting by Scott in the first-grade room at Public School No. 26 on Martindale Avenue. The reporter for the *Indianapolis Star* wrote that Scott had shown much originality in the theme and treatment of his subject. The reporter's interpretation of the mural's theme was:

> His subject is The Old Woman Who Lived in a Shoe and as the woman, he has chosen a typical old colored mammy busily engaged in looking after the affairs of her numerous brood, who of all ages and degrees from babyhood up to long-legged youth, are frolicking gayly along the way. He apparently has undertaken to indicate the happy, lightheartedness characteristic of childhood of the colored race and has accomplished his purpose admirably. His taste in choosing to depict modern life and his own people instead of borrowing from classic models caused approving comment on the part of visitors present.[16]

The second mural completed during the period was unveiled on 7 March 1913 at Public School No. 23. Scott had attended this school, and he painted the mural in his first classroom. The painting was twenty-three feet long and forty inches high and titled *The Fountain of Knowledge.* A newspaper reporter noted that the mural was one of the most beautiful works of its kind. Describing Scott as "the young colored artist, whose work has attracted widespread attention," she offered her interpretation of his mural. She wrote:

> He calls it "The Fountain of Knowledge," and has carried out the idea by representing the teacher and a group of children, whose toys and pastimes typify the different arts and trades of the world. A small boy with a hammer and toyhouse represents the carpentering trade, one child with a tiny boat typifies commerce, while two little girls represent music and dancing. The figures are all of colored children, and range in shade from the very light to the darkest seen in the race.
>
> Mr. Scott's idea was to portray the happy-go-lucky disposition of the colored child, and the fact that the colored child more than that of any other race acquires his knowledge unconsciously. He is not studious by nature; he does not inherit any tendency to study. His life, even under stress of poverty and misfortune, is one happy frolic. And yet he unconsciously absorbs knowledge through no apparent application of his own, until, as the artist expressed it: "All at once he has acquired something." Certainly the picture is the embodiment of the life and gayety of childhood.[17]

In April 1914 Scott returned from a year's study in France and his third trip to Europe. He had studied for four months at the Julian Academy in Paris and eight months with Tanner. Scott submitted two paintings for jury in two exhibitions. A salon in Paris accepted one painting, titled *Le Connaisseur,* while the Royal Academy in London accepted the other painting, *Silver Sun at Boulogne.* It was an outstanding honor to have paintings exhibited in both Paris and London.[18] Scott also painted murals in the Burdsal wing of City Hospital (currently Wishard) in Indianapolis that comprised twenty-six panels, which were from five to forty feet wide and included three hundred figures. The themes that Scott used in these works were the four seasons and biblical subjects. He began work on the murals in early 1915 and completed them in October of that year.[19] Recognition and honors for Scott's outstanding works came from throughout America as well as abroad. The Harmon Foundation was instituted in 1926 to award outstanding achievement in the arts by blacks. In 1928 the foundation presented Scott a special gold medal for distinctive achievement in fine art. In 1931 he received the Julius Rosenwald fellowship for study in Haiti. He was there for a year and painted over one hundred pieces in oil. The president of Haiti purchased ten of Scott's works.[20] The Haiti government honored his work in 1936 with the presentation of the Haitian Officer in the National Order of *Honneur et Merite,* which was equivalent to the French Legion of Honor.[21] In 1943 the Recorder of Deeds Building in Washington, D.C., was selected for a series of murals in which, for the first time, the importance of the black race in the country was stressed as a subject for design. Three hundred sixty designs by 124 artists, including William Scott, were submitted from all over the United States. This was known as the National Anonymous Mural Competition, since many of the designs were not signed. Scott's design of *Frederick Douglass Appealing to President Lincoln* was one of seven winners. Of interest is the fact that Scott was the only black artist to win in the competition. His mural is five feet, ten inches wide and five feet, eight inches high. Scott received $650 for his work.[22]

Due to diabetes, Scott had a leg amputated in 1957, but the operation did not stop him from producing new work or going on lecture tours.[23] He died in Chicago in May 1964 at the age of eighty and was survived by his wife Esther, a daughter Joan Wallace, and four grandchildren.[24]

Although the preservation of his artwork commissioned in his native Indianapolis does not attest to it, Scott left a legacy of art. Listed in *Who Was Who in America,* he has mural decorations in the Fort Wayne, Indiana, courthouse and large frescoes in the Illinois statehouse in Springfield, the Lafayette, Indiana, courthouse, First Presbyterian Church of Chicago, and the People's Finance Corporation Bank in St. Louis. The murals on the walls in the public schools in Indianapolis were painted over or dismantled. There is no record of what was done with Scott's artwork on canvas once they were removed.

Courtesy of John W. Lee

William E. Scott's drawing of his cousin, John William Aaron Scott, was one of many he produced of family members.

Many of Scott's paintings are in private collections throughout the country. They are a testament to an era that Scott shared with two of his midwestern contemporaries, John Hardrick (reared in Indianapolis) and Hale Woodruff (attended John

Herron Art Institute in Indianapolis). Like other black artists, they have left their, sometime silent, thumbprints upon the Hoosier landscape.

Notes

1. Obituary of Edna Augusta Scott, Jan. 1954, Schomburg Center for Research in Black Culture, New York, N.Y.

2. Francis C. Holbrook, "William Edouard Scott," *Southern Workman* (Feb. 1924): 72–73.

3. *Indianapolis News,* 12 Sept. 1903.

4. Holbrook, "William Edouard Scott," 73.

5. *Indianapolis Star,* 17 Nov. 1912.

6. *Chicago Record-Herald,* 26 July 1909.

7. *Indianapolis News,* 9 Dec. 1911.

8. Holbrook, "William Edouard Scott," 24.

9. "Men of the Month," *Crisis* (Mar. 1913): 224.

10. *Indianapolis News,* 9 Dec. 1911.

11. Interview with Mr. and Mrs. John W. Lee, relatives of William E. Scott. There are periods of time written about Scott's travels between Europe and the United States that overlap or conflict on given dates about events that are reported. It was reported that Scott returned to the United States after about fifteen months in Paris, and the reason given for his return was because he had run very short of funds. There was an account of his return in an Indianapolis newspaper, with the headlines proclaiming, "Colored Artist Home from Study in Paris." The article gave general information about his schooling in Indianapolis and in Chicago as well as his art activities in Paris. *Indianapolis News,* 19 Nov. 1910; 9 Dec. 1911.

12. "Men of the Month," 224.

13. Holbrook, "William Edouard Scott," 74.

14. *Indianapolis Star,* 17 Nov. 1912.

15. This researcher's sources, as early as 1924, all indicate 1918 as the year *Rainy Day Etaples* was donated to the John Herron Art Institute; however, I since have found this date to be in error. The *Art Association of Indianapolis Indiana John Herron Art Institute, Annual Report 1912–1913* lists *Rainy Day Etaples* under Accessions. A photograph of Scott's painting is also included in the annual report. *Indianapolis Star,* 9 Mar. 1913.

16. *Indianapolis Star,* 9 Feb. 1913.

17. Ibid., 9 Mar. 1913.

18. *Indianapolis News,* 16 Apr. 1914.

19. *Indianapolis Star,* 31 Oct. 1915.

20. *The West Virginian,* 14 Nov. 1938.

21. *Chicago Defender,* 18 July 1936.

22. *Indianapolis Star,* 2 Apr. 1943.

23. *Chicago Daily Tribune,* 30 Apr. 1960.

24. *Indianapolis Star,* 19 May 1964.

Indiana
African-American
History Sources

Connecting the Dots: The Quest to Gather the History of African-Americans in Indiana

Wilma L. Gibbs

During the fall of 1983 a group of scholars met on the Purdue University campus for the Conference on the Study and Teaching of Afro-American History sponsored by the American Historical Association. This group, which included some of the most prominent historians and educators in their fields, was on a mission. The mission was to assess and evaluate the field of African-American history—its past, present, and future.

At one conference session John Hope Franklin shared his views about the field. He considered four generations of scholarship of unequal lengths in African-American history. The first he dated from 1882 and the publication of *History of the Negro Race in America* by George Washington Williams through the 1909 publication of Booker T. Washington's *The Story of the Negro.* Admitting that it was difficult to characterize the first period, Franklin stated that the common objective of the writers was to define and describe the role of blacks in the life of the nation. As he further pointed out, whether in the integrationist mode of Williams or the accommodationist stance of Washington, historians of the first period were concerned with adaptation and compatibility of African-Americans in the predominantly white world in which they lived.

Franklin dated the second generation of African-American scholarship through 1935. It included the 1915 publication of W. E. B. Du Bois's *The Negro;* the founding of the Association for the Study of Negro Life and History (ASNLH) and the launching of the *Journal of Negro History* (in 1915 and 1916, respectively); and the 1922 publication of Carter G. Woodson's *The Negro in Our History.* Unlike the first generation, this group boasted academically trained historians. Woodson, the undisputed leader among them, was very much interested in the promotion of Negro history. In 1926 he began Negro History Week; fifty years later it became Afro-American History Month. Also at the early annual meetings of the ASNLH, there were always several sessions devoted to the art of teaching African-American history to elementary and secondary students.

Franklin's third generation began with the appearance of W. E. B. Du Bois's *Black Reconstruction* in 1935 and ended with the close of the 1960s. Like their colleagues of the second generation, the historians of this era were academically trained, many of them at a handful of midwestern and eastern universities. They exploited less the achievements of African-Americans and tended to put the field of study into a larger context. Certainly this is the case with Emma Lou Thornbrough's *The Negro in Indiana before 1900: The Study of a Minority* and *Since Emancipation: A Short History of Indiana Negroes,* both published during this period. Franklin linked the historians' efforts to integrate African-American history into the body of the nation's history to the fight of black students to gain access to graduate departments of history in predominantly white universities and to the fight of African-Americans to gain admission to the mainstream of American life.

The fourth and final generation, according to Franklin, began about 1970. This period marked an accelerated intensity in the study of African-American history, as well as the introduction of approaches that led to new interpretations. The range of subjects was broad-based, spanning the Colonial period, Reconstruction, and the twentieth century.

Moving beyond Franklin's observations, the various papers presented at the conference could be divided into two sections. One would encompass the field of study itself and the other would incorporate the peripheral concerns pertaining to the treatment of African-American history, including teaching, researching, and funding. The latter category was comprised of papers on black history courses and textbooks, black history and the community, and integrating the teaching of black history into American history. The first category, the whole field of African-American history, for purposes of the conference, was divided into three broad topics—slavery, emancipation, and urban studies. It is within the context of these broad topics that I frame my remarks about the development of scholarship in Indiana African-American history.

A recent survey of printed materials related to the history of African-Americans in Indiana at the Indiana Historical Society suggests trends that coincide with Franklin's observations. Of the 135 titles reviewed, slightly less than half were Indiana-specific. It is necessary to note that at least 10 of the titles are speeches pertaining to slavery that were published during the 1850s and 1860s. About half of the Indiana titles were published during Franklin's fourth generation of scholarship, i.e., since 1970.

The unifying factor of the existence of African-Americans in the United States prior to 1865 was slavery. Indiana black residents during the 1850s were sandwiched between the push of the Hoosier state and the pull of the national agenda. Moreover, they were affected by the passage of Article 13, the exclusion clause of the 1851 Indiana Constitution, and other restrictive laws, many of which are delineated in Earl McDonald's 1931

Indiana Magazine of History article, "The Negro in Indiana before 1881." No less repressive were several national measures enacted during the decade, including the passage of the Fugitive Slave Law and the Supreme Court ruling in the Dred Scott case. Though subjective in tone, McDonald's article contains useful information about the legal status of blacks in Indiana prior to an 1881 amendment to the 1851 constitution.

Two useful titles that can serve as models for the Indiana African-American Slavery Studies period are Leon Litwack's *North of Slavery: The Negro in the Free States, 1790–1860* and, to a lesser extent, *The Free Black in Urban America, 1800–1850* by Leonard Curry. *North of Slavery* puts into a national context many of the subjects treated in Emma Lou Thornbrough's *The Negro in Indiana before 1900.* Though Litwack is more zealous in his treatment of abolitionism and the federal government's response to blacks in the free states, and Thornbrough in her observation of population changes and migratory patterns, both volumes present a wealth of information about the socioeconomic and political conditions for northern blacks. The authors broach subjects and identify topics and issues for further and more in-depth study.

Gwendolyn Crenshaw's exhibition catalog, *"Bury Me in a Free Land": The Abolitionist Movement in Indiana, 1816–1865,* is a grand introduction to the study of the antislavery movement in Indiana in general, and, more specifically, the Underground Railroad. A well-documented source, it, along with Tom Hamm's *The Anti-Slavery Movement in Henry County: A Study of the Local Abolitionists* and Levi Coffin's *Reminiscences,* could serve as a point of departure for a book-length manuscript on statewide abolitionist activities. The catalog is a refreshing change from the folksy, mythical, whimsical, and story-driven tales that currently punctuate the history of the Underground Railroad in Indiana.

The rise and fall and resurrection of the colonization movement within Indiana is a subject that has received limited attention in various works, but certainly merits its own volume. A

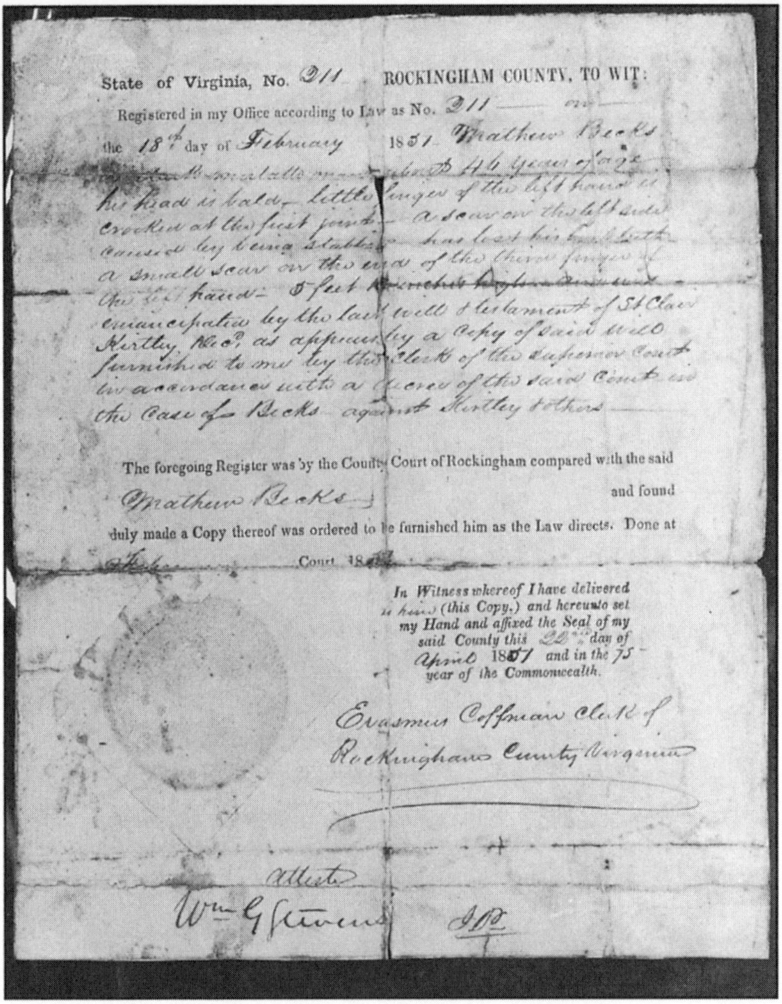

State of Virginia, No. 211 ROCKINGHAM COUNTY, TO WIT:

Registered in my Office according to Law as No. 211 on
the 18th day of February 1851 Mathew Becks
a mulatto man about 46 years of age
his head is bald, little finger of the left hand is
crooked at the first joint, a scar on the left side
caused by being stabbed has lost his [illegible] teeth
a small scar on the end of the three finger of
the left hand 5 feet [illegible] inches high [illegible]
emancipated by the last will & testament of St Clair
Kirtley, Dec'd, as appears by a copy of said will
furnished to me by the Clerk of the Superior Court
in accordance with a decree of the said Court in
the case of Becks against Kirtley & others

The foregoing Register was by the County Court of Rockingham compared with the said
Mathew Becks and found
duly made a Copy thereof was ordered to be furnished him as the Law directs. Done at
Feb[illegible] Court 1851

In Witness whereof I have delivered to him (this Copy.) and hereunto set my Hand and affixed the Seal of my said County this 22nd day of April 1851 and in the 75 year of the Commonwealth.

Erasmus Coffman Clerk of
Rockingham County Virginia

Attest
Wm G Stevens J.P.

IHS

Matthew Becks was emancipated in Rockingham County, Virginia, in 1851 before migrating to Rush County, Indiana. His emancipation record includes a physical description of Becks and states that he was freed by the last will and testament of St. Clair Kirtley.

study of colonization could help put into context the pro and con sentiments of Hoosiers from the time period between the 1816 and the 1851 state constitutions. Just as important is an examination of the state and national Negro convention movements as they pertained to black Hoosiers. Philip Foner and George Walker's book, *Proceedings of the Black State Conventions, 1840–1865*, covers the evolution of the state convention movement. The authors include Indiana activity in a chronological listing of proceedings.

Several articles have appeared in recent years that have furthered the development of the Slave Studies period. Many of these articles are contained in *Black History News & Notes*, the

IHS C2170

The Union Literary Institute in Randolph County, Indiana, was one of a few post-secondary schools in the state that permitted blacks to enroll before the Civil War.

newsletter of the Black History Program of the Indiana Historical Society. Of particular note are Earline Rae Ferguson's "In Pursuit of the Full Enjoyment of Liberty and Happiness: Blacks in Antebellum Indianapolis, 1820–1860," Lori Jacobi's "More than a Church: The Educational Role of the African Methodist Episcopal Church in Indiana, 1844–1861," and Xenia Cord's "Black Rural Settlements in Indiana before 1860."

Cord did not enter into uncharted lands in 1987 when she explored black rural settlements, although hers was the first effort to synthesize a large group of these Indiana communities into one piece of writing. Thirty years earlier, Edward Conkling completed a masters thesis at the University of Chicago entitled "Roberts Settlement: A Mixed-Blood Agricultural Community in Indiana." Stephen Vincent liked the topic so well that as an undergraduate at Indiana University he wrote his B. A. thesis on the emergence of the Robertses and Roberts Settlement. Expanding and thoroughly examining his topic, he recently completed his dissertation, "African-Americans in the Rural Midwest: The Origins and Evolution of Beech and Roberts Settlements, ca. 1760–1900." *Lyles Station, Indiana, Yesterday and Today* by Carl Lyles recounts the history of an agrarian community in Gibson County in southwestern Indiana. Jacqueline Cortez's *Contributions in Black and Red: Local History of Negro Settlement in Southwestern Indiana and Illinois* identifies black rural communities in Knox County. Also Coy Robbins, who has done extensive research on African-Americans in Washington County, has in print two small volumes on blacks in Hamilton and Morgan counties.

Emancipation, the historical interval that attaches slavery to urbanization, is a transitional linkage. In noting the growth of black churches, colleges, clubs, and fraternal organizations, Eric Foner has concluded in a 1982 review in *Reviews in American History* that the period "gave birth to the modern black community, whose roots lay deep in slavery, but whose structure reflected the consequences of emancipation." The printed sources for the period tend to reflect the effort to promote a sense of community. To establish background for the emancipation period one can look at the standard-bearer, *The Negro in Indiana before 1900*. Beyond Thornbrough's analysis of population changes between 1865 and 1900, there has been very little written on the impact of demographic trends of African-Americans in the state for that time period. If there is consolation in comparable neglect, *nothing* has been written that addresses the population explosion of blacks within the state after World War II. A recent *Black History News & Notes* article by Arnold Cooper, "Reverend John H. Clay and the 1879 Exodus to Greencastle, Indiana: A Case Study of AME Leadership," gives an account of a North Carolina migration to one western Indiana town. Similar studies need to be written about the 1879 migration to other parts of Indiana including Clay, Hendricks, Montgomery, and Shelby counties.

A theme that crosses the historical literature about the period is the black Hoosier's existence within the context of a segregated society, just one step the other side of slavery. The biographies and the institutional histories that denote the Emancipation Studies period illuminate the mood. Indiana-connected individuals of the period who have been the subject of book-length studies include George Knox and "Major" Taylor. Madam C. J. Walker was the subject of a young adult biography that was completed last year. The author, A'Lelia Bundles, who served as the researcher for a book that Alex Haley contracted to write about the businesswoman, now plans to write a definitive work. George Knox's autobiography, serialized in his newspaper, the *Freeman*, revealed that he was a former slave who came to Indiana, became a successful barber, and was active in Republican party politics. Willard Gatewood edited the autobiography and added an introduction to it. *Slave and Freeman* was published in 1979. In 1987 Englishman Andrew Ritchie relied heavily on Marshall Walter Taylor's 1928 autobiography and European newspapers to chronicle the story of the native-born

Madam C. J. Walker Collection, IHS C2137

The Senate Avenue Young Men's Christian Association dedicated its building in 1913. During a week-long program, Booker T. Washington gave the dedicatory speech on 13 July. (Left to right:) George Knox, Madam C. J. Walker, F. B. Ransom, Booker T. Washington, Alexander Manning, Dr. Joseph Ward, R. W. Bullock, and Thomas A. Taylor.

Hoosier in *Major Taylor: The Extraordinary Career of a Champion Bicycle Racer.* Autobiographical notes about the life of Moses Broyles, a former slave and minister who migrated to Indianapolis, are contained in his book, *The History of the Second Baptist Church.*

A bit of political history can be gleaned from Ronald Snell's 1972 dissertation, "Indiana's Black Representatives: The Rhetoric of the Black Republican Legislators from 1880 to 1896." Black newspapers of the time period are a rich source for social history. Specifically, the *Freeman* and the *Colored World* (dating from the mid-1880s), and the *Recorder* (from 1895) are useful.

Courtesy of the Indiana State Museum

Major Taylor with his wife Daisy and daughter Sydney, ca. 1907

Ruth Crocker's dissertation, "Sympathy and Science: The Settlement Movement in Gary and Indianapolis to 1930," is a well-documented source that contains information about the development of social-service agencies located in both cities. Judy

IHS A70

The Flanner Guild (later Flanner House) in Indianapolis and the Stewart House in Gary were established to help alleviate the stress of a black, rural, and migrant population moving to the urban North. Both agencies developed various self-help programs to respond to the health, social, and educational needs of their clients.

Jolley Mohraz includes Indianapolis as one of the three cities of examination in *The Separate Problem: Case Studies of Black Education in the North,* and Stanley Warren elaborates on school segregation and the development of Crispus Attucks High School in Indianapolis in a two-part article in *Black History News & Notes.*

Women's history sources for the period include Ferguson's articles that have appeared in *Black History News & Notes* and the *Indiana Magazine of History* pertaining to Lillian Thomas Fox and the work of the Woman's Improvement Club. Another source is Darlene Clark Hine's book, *When the Truth Is Told: A History of Black Women's Culture and Community in Indiana, 1875–1950,* that was an outgrowth of her work with the National Council of Negro Women, Indianapolis Section. Her association with two members of the organization, Virtea Downey and Shirley Herd, led to the Black Women in the Middle West Project, an effort to collect primary source materials in Indiana and Illinois during the 1980s.

If the Emancipation Studies period is characterized by the freedman adjusting to his environment under the shield of his segregated communities and the development of those communities through organizational efforts, then urbanization incapsulates everything that occurred once he stepped outside that protected environment. The urbanization period captured the movement of southern migrants to the urban North. Although migration started earlier, this period is dated from about 1920. Robert Grant's *The Black Man Comes to the City: A Documentary Account from the Great Migration to the Great Depression* is a good general introduction to the topic. The Indiana version has not been written. Another useful general source for the time period is Nancy Weiss' *Farewell to the Party of Lincoln: Black Politics in the Age of FDR*. Indiana-specific sources for this period are few and varied. Two studies germane to Indianapolis are Dallas Daniels's *History of the Federation of Associated Clubs* and Clyde Bolden's thesis, "Indiana Avenue: Black Entertainment Boulevard." *Big Steel: Black Politics and Corporate Power in Gary, Indiana*, by Edward Greer, describes the state of affairs under Mayor Richard G. Hatcher. Emma Lou Thornbrough's article on public accommodations in Indiana that appeared in the December 1987 issue of the *Indiana Magazine of History* gives a history of the topic to 1963.

Most of what can be termed homespun histories overlap time periods. Many of them begin with the antebellum era, and after two pages they reach the urbanization period. Darrel Bigham's excellent work, *We Ask Only a Fair Trial: A History of the Black Community of Evansville, Indiana*, provides a model for local histories.

There is much work to be done in Indiana African-American history. What is needed most can be summed up in two words—

researching and writing. Specifically there is a need for local and state institutional histories of the Indianapolis Urban League; Indianapolis chapter of the National Association for the Advancement of Colored People; Flanner House; the *Indianapolis Recorder;* National Council of Negro Women, Indianapolis Section; Indiana State Federation of Colored Women's Clubs; and the Senate Avenue YMCA. Also there is a need for the publication of biographies, especially about individuals who have national and international reputations such as Madam C. J. Walker and Wes Montgomery. The recent release of *The Art of Archibald Motley, Jr.,* serves as a reminder of the need for extended biographies on Indiana-connected artists John Hardrick, William Edouard Scott, and Hale Woodruff. Also needed are general histories on specific themes: civil rights, black Hoosiers in the Civil War, and the interconnections between residents of various rural communities. It is necessary to note that until the very specific subjects receive treatment, it will be much more difficult for researchers to complete interpretive and comparative studies. For example, it would be interesting to see a comparative study of the political, economic, and social stratifications of African-Americans in Gary and Indianapolis who witnessed the election of Indiana's first black mayor and the inception of Uni-Gov, respectively during the 1960s. A basis for the Gary section of the comparative study can be found in *Big Steel: Black Politics and Corporate Power in Gary, Indiana.* The Indianapolis contribution to the study remains in the repositories of institutions and individuals. In addition to more expanded topics and better documented writings, two projects would certainly facilitate the work of researchers: indexing of the *Indianapolis Recorder* and other pertinent newspapers and the publication of a source that describes materials available at the county level useful for exploring the history of African-Americans.

Obviously, as archivists and librarians cannot afford the luxury of having resources and not making them accessible, historians cannot simply research and write without giving thought to the dissemination of their work—the public history aspect. The lack of available secondary sources can impact the promotion of history to the general public. For example, rarely will media projects rely on anything other than secondary sources.

The history of African-Americans in Indiana is contained within the collective memories, public and private repositories, and attics and basements of the rural, urban, and suburban dwellers of the state and beyond. Spanning the antebellum period until the present, the historical bits of material found in these places provide information about individuals, events, and activities pertaining to blacks in Indiana from Gary to Free Bridge and from Terre Haute to Richmond. The information gives evidence of historical occurrences and watershed periods, putting into a national context the history of the state's African-American population. By connecting the dots, a coherent picture will emerge.

(This lecture was presented at the 1992 annual meeting of the Indiana Association of Historians.)

Indiana Applications to the Cherokee Restitution Appropriation of 1906: A Little-Known Source for Black Genealogy

Xenia E. Cord

In 1906 the settlement of three general jurisdiction cases brought by the Eastern Cherokees against the United States government resulted in legislation providing for restitution to those Cherokees who had been deprived of real and personal property as a part of the forced resettlement of the 1830s. Anyone of Cherokee ancestry was invited to apply for consideration. In Indiana a great many of those who applied were descendants of early black settlers from North Carolina and other southeastern states; they were people whose family oral histories included Cherokee elements. The circumstances surrounding their presence in Indiana and their application to the fund should be of genealogical as well as historical interest.

At the beginning of the Civil War 11,262 free blacks were living in Indiana, the majority of whom, like their white counterparts, were migrating pioneers from the Upland South who had come to Indiana in response to cheap land and increased opportunities.[1] Another tremendous attraction of the state was its legal ban on involuntary servitude. Despite the southern bias of many of its white citizens and the legislature's increasingly restrictive posture toward black settlement, Indiana in its preindustrial period represented something of a haven for free blacks leaving the slave states. While some of the blacks enumerated in Indiana's 1860 census were recently manumitted or emancipated slaves, and a small percentage were escaped slaves, the great majority were freeborn, and many were Indiana natives whose families were some of the early settlers of the state.

Following the pattern of Indiana's development, early black pioneers settled along the southern reaches of the Wabash in present-day Vigo and Gibson counties, in Dubois, Orange, Washington, and Jackson counties, those counties below what was known as the Ten O'Clock Treaty line, and along the White and Whitewater River areas of eastern Indiana, in the area from Cincinnati to Winchester known as "the gore." In these areas they settled in loosely knit cooperative agricultural groupings, as did their white neighbors. They lived as they had migrated, among friends and family members from their previous home areas.[2]

Many of the black settlers had southern Quaker neighbors, a circumstance that often may have been as spontaneous and coincidental as it was conscious. Quakers, including southern Quakers, have long had a reputation as antislavery proponents who were interested in resettling blacks in states and territories where slavery was not allowed. That some southern Quakers were deeply committed to rescuing blacks from slavery is well documented, but the relationship between free black families and Quakers in the South and the impulses that triggered their migration together or separately to Indiana have not been investigated. Not all members of the Society of Friends were active in the antislavery movement, and a moral aversion to slavery did not signal automatic acceptance of blacks as neighbors and friends. In Indiana, in fact, Quakers were sharply divided over the issue, and the conflict over commitment led to the formation of a faction that called itself the Anti-Slavery Friends.

Many southern Quakers who migrated with their coreligionists to Indiana to form new congregations may also have been tolerant of their black neighbors for economic rather than altruistic reasons. However the association was created, and however uneasy it may have been, settlement in areas contiguous to Quaker settlements seems to have provided passive acceptance of the black rural communities that helped to ease their establishment. Despite Indiana's relatively hostile climate, which intensified sharply in the decade preceding the Civil War, the settlements grew, their populations swelled by infusions of friends and relatives fleeing the South even as earlier black settlers opted to move northward into Michigan and Upper Canada.

Among the Carolina black families who migrated early to the states formed out of the Northwest Territory were many who could document freeborn status from before the Revolution. Many were also members of a complexly interrelated group of freeborn people constrained by North Carolina law to their own society, who left that state in response to increasingly restrictive legislation governing the livelihoods and movements of free blacks. Any number of those who moved to Indiana between 1820 and the eve of the Civil War were able to name their ancestors back to the middle of the eighteenth century. For instance, the Roberts family, an extended group from Chatham County, North Carolina, settled very early in Orange County. Among these early settlers was Ishmael Roberts, a Revolutionary War veteran of Private Shepard's Company, Tenth North Carolina Regiment, who had received a government land grant for his service.[3] Another who saw similar service was Thomas Archie, whose daughter married a son of Ishmael Roberts and moved to Orange County in 1824. Robertses were also responsible for helping to found settlements in Rush, Vigo, and Hamilton counties, and their extensive correspondence, family papers, and genealogy have been the subject of several studies.[4] No fewer than thirty-four people from Indiana with the Roberts surname later filed for consideration of claims under the Cherokee Restitution Act.

Others whose free heritage was a matter of family record include Edmund Pettiford, born in 1794, who came to Grant County in 1858 to join his children, and whose ten generations of descendants have been traced to the present.[5] Edmund Pettiford's wife, Sarah Carter, claimed to be three-fourths Cherokee, and in 1852 their daughter Clarinda had a child by a Cherokee named Osborne Giles. Markus Hammond, a Cherokee born in the eighteenth century, was the father of Thomas Hammond, an immigrant to Indiana, and grandfather of Mary Hammond Roberts of Kokomo. Gertrude Gaskin of Kokomo could document that her mother was freeborn in Randolph County, North Carolina, in 1837, and that her maternal grandfather was a white man; on her father's side she claimed black and Cherokee heritage. Many of these families had a history of interracial involvement, however informal, that included both white and Indian connections.

Following the Civil War the rapid influx of blacks from the emancipated South diluted to some extent Indiana's concentration of mixed heritage free blacks, but for the most part the rural settlements continued to maintain and to extend their rather exclusive interfamilial relationships, creating a largely undocumented genealogical puzzle. Only the most meticulously maintained family records, the memories of the living elderly, and those documents generated by law and circumstance exist to aid researchers in untangling a complicated heritage. Considering the paucity of sources for black genealogy in Indiana, new documents that come to light should be enthusiastically explored. One such source is the material generated by applicants to the United States Court of Claims between 1906 and 1909 in the matter of the distribution of more than one million dollars appropriated by Congress, to be paid as restitution to the Eastern Cherokees.

These documents, which exist in the manuscript original and on microfilm, are generally entitled "Eastern Cherokee Applications of the United States Court of Claims, 1906–1909," consisting of 348 rolls of film or 175 linear feet of shelf storage at the National Archives, and the companion "Records Relating to the Enrollment of Eastern Cherokees by Guion Miller, 1908–1910," consisting of 12 rolls of microfilm. The smaller group of records includes the alphabetical index of all claimants (by their English names) and the application number given to each claim. Also included in this series are depositions taken in the field during the summer of 1908, several Cherokee census enrollments, and other miscellaneous material.[6]

The following is a brief description of the circumstances of the distribution. In 1830 Congress passed a Removal Bill aimed at forcing the Cherokee Nation and other native groups out of what is now the southeastern United States. For the next eight years the Cherokee Nation argued against the forced removal, bringing to bear on the government arguments illustrating its social, educational, and governmental institutions. Because of a complex series of circumstances involving states' rights, unrelated Indian insurrections, and political and military personalities dedicated to eradication of "the Indian problem," the Cherokee arguments failed. In 1838 nearly seventeen thousand Cherokees were forcibly removed from their ancestral home on the East Coast, although the majority of Cherokees had not participated in the 1835 removal treaty at New Echota. For a variety of reasons many Cherokees were not found and expelled from the Carolinas, Tennessee, and Georgia with the rest. The citizenship status and land ownership rights of those who remained behind were a legal dilemma that persisted for the next half a century. The group, which called itself Eastern Cherokee, considered itself a tribal unit but was not accorded official recognition by the federal government. Without this recognition the Eastern Cherokees had no status, either as government dependents or as citizens. Because the federal government did not recognize them as citizens, neither did the states in which they lived (a condition that remained unchanged until 1924). Unrecognized as tribal members by the United States government, and without legal citizenship in the country or the states in which they resided, members of the band of Eastern Cherokees and those informally considered to be Cherokee by themselves and others suffered numerous abuses, many of them resulting in the confiscation or theft of personal property, livestock, and real estate. The Cherokee Nation and the Eastern Cherokee band finally instituted a series of suits against the United States, claiming grievances arising from the two removal treaties: the 1835 Treaty of New Echota, ratified by Congress in 1836, and the Treaty of Washington ten years later.[7]

In 1905 the court of claims found in favor of the Cherokees, necessitating the compiling of a list of those eligible to receive a share of the award created by congressional legislation. Guion Miller of the Interior Department was appointed special commissioner for the court of claims, empowered to receive and investigate the claims of applicants and to compile the final roll of eligible applicants. The fact that claimants had to show participation in the treaties of 1836 and 1846, or descent from a person enrolled at those times or in any other contemporary Cherokee census, did not deter many applicants whose heritage was undocumented or uncertain. Among those who filed claims were several hundred black residents of Indiana, chiefly those from the east-central part of the state.

Among the 45,847 applications (representing about 90,000 individuals) eventually filed with the government by 1909, just over 30,000 were accepted, the majority of the claimants living west of the Mississippi River, where the United States government had forced the Cherokee nation to settle. Those claims that were rejected included almost the entire group of claimants from east-central Indiana. Critical to the success of an application was the listing of an ancestor who had been enrolled previously as a member of the Cherokee Nation. If the applicant could not name or document his or her supposed Cherokee connection, or if the named Cherokee ancestor had not been enrolled as a condition of his or her Cherokee status, the application was rejected.

In the antebellum United States, when a decennial census was taken the United States Bureau of the Census employed census takers locally to count whites, blacks, and (in the South) slaves. The Department of the Interior, and later the Bureau of Indian Affairs, enumerated the Indians and compiled the statistics that appeared in a separate census. In the 1810 and 1820 North Carolina manuscript census on microfilm, no racial designation is given except for a diacritical hash mark next to the names of those who were freeborn blacks, and their enumeration by age groupings and sex in the columns under "slave," since the forms did not provide any place to record those neither white nor slave. By 1830 the notation "fcp" for "free colored person" appears by the names of those enumerated blacks who were not slave. Children of racially mixed heritage would likely be considered of the same race as the families in which they lived, and would be counted by whatever governmental agency was responsible for counting that race.

Even among Indians the status of blacks was often unclear. A census of Eastern Cherokees in 1825 showed designations for native Cherokees, white men and white women married into the nation, and Negro slaves, but no category for blacks married into the nation.[8] And yet black/Indian relationships were common, and southern Indian tribes were well known for harboring black fugitives from slavery. Even earlier, during the numerous repatriation efforts insisted upon by the United States government in peace treaties, Indian tribes frequently refused to return Negroes living among them to a life of slavery.[9] Despite a lack of formal enumeration, individuals who could claim both black and Cherokee heritage were common. Among the black families who later migrated to Indiana there was ample evidence of Cherokee ancestry in family oral histories.

Black families living outside the Cherokee Nation who knew that certain of their numbers were at least part Cherokee in heritage had no reason to give that information to the census takers, who at any rate would probably not have asked for it. In addition, because of the uncertain nature of the citizenship status of Cherokees in North Carolina, it may have been advisable for those of mixed ancestry to be enumerated among the free blacks. As curtailed as their livelihoods and activities were by the growing strictures of state law, at midcentury free blacks were still accorded citizenship in that state. So although a great many of the Indiana black claimants to the Cherokee Restitution Fund of 1906 produced historical oral information and corroborating testimony from elderly friends attesting to their North Carolina Cherokee heritage, the liaisons were apparently casual or undocumented in any legal way, and thus the information was considered flawed.

However, the validity of Cherokee heritage claims is not at issue here. What is of primary importance is the ancestral information provided by the claimants to the restitution fund, and the interfamily relationships detailed by the claim forms, the subsequent testimony, and by investigators who dealt with the accumulated records. The initial applications asked a series of twenty-one questions in which the applicant was to detail his or her ancestry, including maternal and paternal grandparents, parents, aunts and uncles on both sides, and siblings. Dates of birth and death for each were requested. Places of residence, past and current, and dates of removal were asked, as well as place of residence in 1851, when the critical enrollments were completed. The claimant was asked, "By what right do you claim to share? If you claim through more than one relative living in 1851, set forth each claim separately [question 7]." Finally, respondents were asked to detail their grandparents' paternal and maternal ancestors back to 1835 [question 21]. Each application was signed by a notary and attested by two witnesses who swore to (or affirmed, in the case of Quaker witnesses) the number of years they had known the applicant.

Applications received by the court of claims between August 1906 and May 1909 were assigned a number according to the date of receipt; also filed with each claim was any subsequent correspondence from either the claimant or his agent or from the special investigator's staff, unclaimed rejection notices, and legal documents such as powers of attorney and last wills and testaments executed during the three-year period. Eventually the applications were indexed in alphabetical order, giving the English name of the applicant, his or her place of residence, and the application number.[10]

As the claims were received their information was checked against the various Cherokee rolls previously compiled by the Department of the Interior; among these were the Eastern Cherokee census of 1835, the Chapman, Drennen, and "Old Settler" rolls of 1851, the Siler roll of 1854, and the Hester roll of 1884. The application numbers of successful claimants were cross-referenced with the names of the ancestors on the earlier rolls. For those whose Cherokee heritage was in doubt, including a great percentage of the black applicants from Indiana, additional written testimony was often sought before the decision was made to reject the claim. The documents generated by this research were filed with each application, as were notations on the application covers giving the application numbers for related applicants. It is this information, together with that given by the claimants, that provides the greatest potential for genealogical research.

There is no clear information on the manner in which the eventual claimants learned of the restitution fund, or how they obtained the initial application forms, but it can be assumed that some sort of account would have been carried by local newspapers. Since the applications had to be notarized, members of the legal profession were probably also involved. For instance, it appears from the documentary evidence that many, if not all, of the claimants from Grant and Howard counties were guided in their applications by John R. Hadley, an attorney from Marion. Whether he stimulated the initial interest among the black residents of Grant County by bringing the reparations to their attention is not clear; certainly among local extended families his legal involvement was considerable, judging by the number of applications authorizing him to represent the applicant. Additionally, he represented family members in Howard County, and his name appears on some Grant County claim forms for persons having relatives in Randolph County as well.[11]

In one way or another, several hundred black Indiana residents heard of the fund and applied. The applications were to be submitted by September 1907. Some examples of the applications submitted suggest the activities surrounding the application process and the extent to which the early free black families in Indiana were interrelated. Applications were sent from Grant County on 29 January 1907, including those from relatives Jeremiah Shoecraft, Jane Wallace, Elmer Jones, and Sarah J. Weaver, and also from James T. Pettiford and his daughter Marcia Burden. On the microfilm it is evident from the handwriting that all of these applications were filled out by the same person, possibly Hadley or a clerk in his office. In the next month several of these claimants received similar letters asking why their ancestors were not on the Cherokee rolls, and asking if they or their ancestors were ever slaves. If the answer was yes, they were to state whether they were held by whites or Indians.

At age eighty-five, the Reverend Jeremiah Shoecraft was one of the oldest applicants. Shoecraft's application, No. 15914, "(f)or share of money appropriated for the Eastern Cherokee Indians by the Act of Congress approved June 30, 1906, in accordance with the decrees of the Court of Claims of May 18, 1905, and May 28, 1906," was received 31 January 1907. Written apparently in the handwriting of J. R. Hadley, the application says Shoecraft claimed the right to share through himself and "Silas Shoecraft, Born 1781 - in Nt. C, and his [Silas's] Mother Bicia Nickens, a fullblood Cherokee Indian—born in N.C. + died there in 1832, and her husband—Wm. Shoecraft, a full blood Indian—born in N.C. in 1739 + died there in 1845."

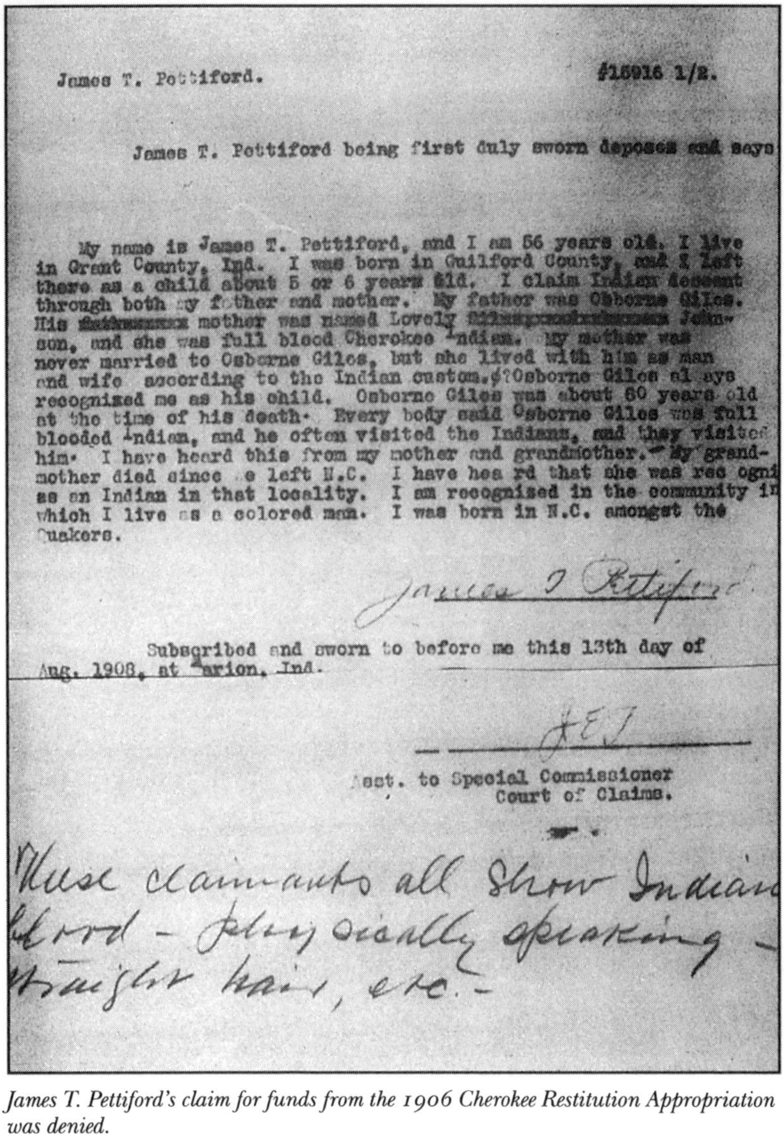

James T. Pettiford. #15916 1/2.

James T. Pettiford being first duly sworn deposes and says:

My name is James T. Pettiford, and I am 56 years old. I live in Grant County, Ind. I was born in Guilford County, and I left there as a child about 5 or 6 years old. I claim Indian descent through both my father and mother. My father was Osborne Giles. His xxxxxxxx mother was named Lovely xxxxxxxxxxxx John-son, and she was full blood Cherokee Indian. My mother was never married to Osborne Giles, but she lived with him as man and wife according to the Indian custom.¢?Osborne Giles always recognized me as his child. Osborne Giles was about 60 years old at the time of his death. Every body said Osborne Giles was full blooded Indian, and he often visited the Indians, and they visited him. I have heard this from my mother and grandmother. My grand-mother died since we left N.C. I have heard that she was recogni as an Indian in that locality. I am recognized in the community in which I live as a colored man. I was born in N.C. amongst the Quakers.

James T Pettiford

Subscribed and sworn to before me this 13th day of Aug. 1908, at Marion, Ind.

JET

Asst. to Special Commissioner
Court of Claims.

These claimants all show Indian blood - physically speaking - straight hair, etc. -

Courtesy of the National Archives

James T. Pettiford's claim for funds from the 1906 Cherokee Restitution Appropriation was denied.

According to his oral history, Jeremiah Shoecraft was the seventh of twelve children of Silas Shoecraft, Sr., and his wife Polly (Mary) Jestin, whose grandfather, Jonathan Baptiste, was born in England. His siblings were Abraham, William, Silas, Jr., John, Starke, Sarah, Charlotte, Rebecca, Mary, Peggy, and Lauretta or Henrietta; in 1907 Jeremiah was the only one surviving. His father, Silas, Sr., was born in 1781 in Hertford County, North Carolina, a son of William E. "Billy" Shoecraft, who was born in 1739. Jeremiah, who attended his grandfather's funeral, said Billy Shoecraft died at the age of 106. Billy Shoecraft's wife was Bicia or Bicey Nickens, claimed by the family to be a Cherokee Indian doctor. Family depositions say Bicia was born and died in Guilford County, North Carolina. Jeremiah's application gave the names of his aunts and uncles and indicated that his parents immigrated to Fountain City in Wayne County, Indiana. He gave the names of his eleven siblings and briefly described his role as a preacher to the Miami Indians, a vocation that was at least in part the reason he settled in Grant County.

Also applying from Grant County were Jane (Mitchell) Jones Wallace, the daughter of Jeremiah's sister Rebecca (Shoecraft) Mitchell Jones, Jane's son Elmer Jones, and Jane's daughter Sarah Jones Weaver. Information in their applications indicates that Jane and her first husband lived briefly in Parke County, Indiana, and that he died in 1865 while serving in the United States Army. Elmer Jones applied later on behalf of his seven children, who ranged in age from six to twenty-five, and formally appointed Hadley to represent him. The applications give a clear view of Hadley's financial interest in the success of the process, since each claimant agreed to give him a percentage of any money received. Sarah Weaver also applied later on behalf of her five children, who were ages ten to twenty. The cover of Sarah Weaver's application lists nineteen claim numbers of related applicants, and this research project has located fifteen more, not including dependent children. Other claimants in this extended and related family, in addition to those thirty-four, included several of Jeremiah's cousins through his uncle William Tatum Shoecraft, and nephews through his brothers Abraham and Silas, Jr. Among these were claimants from the

Richmond and Winchester areas who insisted their heritage did not include any black ancestors. They based their claims on the fact that Jeremiah's brother Silas, Jr., a blacksmith, successfully prosecuted a white man for a debt at a time when blacks in Indiana were not allowed to take a white to court.[12] According to family history, two whites who had known Silas in North Carolina swore he was an Indian, not a black man, and on this testimony he was able to proceed to win his suit.

Another Grant County claimant was James T. Pettiford, who may have had one of the better claims to Cherokee ancestry. In 1908 Clarinda Pettiford Evans, daughter of Edmund and Sarah Carter Pettiford, gave a deposition supporting James Pettiford, stating that she was his mother and Osborne Giles of North Carolina was James Pettiford's father, and that Giles was a Cherokee.[13] James Pettiford also claimed through his mother's mother, relying on family history that Sarah Carter Pettiford was three-fourths Cherokee. Edith Weaver Pettiford, a sister-in-law of Clarinda Pettiford Evans, also testified. James had six children; he filed on behalf of two, and his daughter Marcia Burden and his sons Allwill and Albert filed for themselves and their children.

By March 1907 the Commissioner of Indian Affairs, Department of the Interior, had sent acknowledgment forms notifying the applicants of their application numbers and stating that they would be contacted if additional information was needed. Toward the end of the summer several of the claimants filed supplemental applications for their dependent children. And then they waited. Although not all of the correspondence is included on the microfilms, there is evidence that some of these claimants became restive and wrote to see if and when funds would be forthcoming. In December 1907 and again in July 1908, for instance, Marcia Burden asked what progress was being made on the claims. No replies are recorded.

Apparently there was enough question in the minds of the researchers at the court of claims to warrant additional testimony on many of the Indiana applications, and in August 1908 a deputy investigator for the court of claims, J. Edward Taylor, was sent to Indiana to take depositions and testimony from those whose claims were in question. Moving rapidly across the state, Taylor took depositions in Richmond, Muncie, Marion, Kokomo, and Noblesville in one week. As a part of that miscellaneous testimony, relatives and friends were enlisted to share their memories about the racial heritage of the still hopeful applicants. Although the uniformity of the responses recorded in the depositions suggests that the deputy summarized and substituted his own wording for that of the deponents, and sometimes even signed the forms for them, the information that was forthcoming is nonetheless valuable from a genealogical and historical point of view.

Responding to standardized questions, the deponents were apparently asked to state what they knew of the heritage of the claimant, and to tell what, if any, was their relationship to that person. The deponents were usually older friends and relatives of the hopeful applicant, some with claims of their own, and their testimony about family interrelationships is an important source for genealogists. They were asked to tell at what age and in what year they personally had left North Carolina, and to say whether the family members in question had ever been slaves and whether they had ever shared as Cherokees in a distribution of government funds. Numerous people came forward at Marion to support the claim of Jeremiah Shoecraft, including Jeremiah himself. In support of his position Jeremiah stated that his father voted and mustered as a white man and attended a white church in North Carolina, and that one of his brothers married not once, but twice, white women who were slave owners in North Carolina. (As a point of history, free blacks in North Carolina did vote and do military service until legislative response to the Gabriel Prosser, Denmark Vesey, and Nat Turner slave insurrections removed those privileges in the 1830s.) Jeremiah Shoecraft also detailed an earlier family genealogy, giving the line of descent for two cousins, grandchildren of Billy Shoecraft through his daughters Tobitha and Sarah. His descriptions of his movements and activities during the latter half of the nineteenth century are an interesting glimpse into the life of a free black in Indiana and North Carolina in the last century.

One of Jeremiah's witnesses was 90-year-old James Robbins, another cousin and the son of Tobitha Shoecraft Robbins. James Robbins restated the belief that the Shoecrafts were Cherokee, not black, and said that he had not applied although eligible, because he thought it was all a "water haul" (a slang expression signifying a fruitless effort, derived from the hauling in of empty fishing nets). Cousins Albert, Alvarian, and William D. Shoecraft gave depositions at Muncie in their own behalf, as did Elias Mitchell, but supported at the same time Jeremiah's claim. At Kokomo, Martha Gammons, who gave her age as 103, testified for Cyrus Dempsey and his father Jimmy, but also said that she knew Jeremiah Shoecraft's father Silas, and his uncle William, and that the Shoecrafts were Indians who married colored persons. Another deponent in Kokomo, William S. Elliott, testified that he knew one of the Shoecrafts in Guilford County where he was born, and that "he was recognized as colored but those who knew him more intimately knew he had Indian blood in him. It was either Jerry or his brother."

Following these depositions the claimants settled down to wait again. On 12 December 1908 Jeremiah Shoecraft dictated a letter to Commissioner Guion Miller, asking again if and when he might expect compensation. The next entry in his file is a letter from J. T. Evans, possibly a nephew or cousin, in response to some undocumented letter from the court of claims received in November. In this final letter Evans informed the court that Jeremiah Shoecraft was dead. The process had outwaited him, and without descendants his claim was moot.

However optimistic the black Indiana applicants, their claims were uniformly rejected. On 28 May 1909 Guion Miller submitted his list of accepted claimants and made his final report to the court. Two weeks later the court approved the distribution of the funds, allowing for anticipated errors, revisions, and disputed rejections. Despite notification that Jeremiah Shoecraft was dead, in June the court of claims sent to Shoecraft a letter explaining that his claim had been rejected, and setting forth the limited conditions under which an exception might be filed. This letter appears in the file because it was returned to Washington by the post office. The filing of exceptions was to be completed by 10 August 1909, and the matter set for hearing on the third Monday in October. No exception was filed on behalf of Shoecraft's estate, but among the claimants mentioned as examples, Sarah Weaver filed an exception on behalf of herself, her five children, and twenty-two others. At the hearing the original recommendation to reject was renewed, because the exceptions filed showed no clerical errors and presented no additional material facts.

The final hearing on the 11,757 exceptions filed from across the country resulted in 610 reversals or additions, and the removal of 44 previously accepted applicants from the rolls. The final tally of successful claimants was 30,820, of whom only 3,436 lived east of the Mississippi River. It appears that none of Indiana's black applicants shared in the restitution funds, but the genealogical treasure they generated as a result of applying remains to be explored by anyone seeking information on this interesting aspect of Indiana's history.

Notes

1. United States Bureau of the Census, *The Statistics of the Population of the United States*, vol. 1 of *Ninth Census, 1870* (Washington, D.C.: Government Printing Office, 1872), 6.

2. Xenia E. Cord, "Black Rural Settlements in Indiana before 1860," *Black History News & Notes* (Feb. 1987): 4–8.

3. See Coy D. Robbins, "Lick Creek Settlement: An Early Black Community in Orange County," ibid. (Feb. 1982): 8–12, and (May 1982): 8, 10–12. In this article

Robbins gives Roberts's military record as it appears on his current cemetery marker and indicates that Roberts entered land in 1824.

4. See, for instance, Edgar C. Conkling, "Roberts Settlement: A Mixed-Blood Agricultural Community in Indiana" (Unpublished M.A. thesis, University of Chicago, 1957) and Stephen Vincent, "The Robertses and Roberts Settlement: Emergence of a Black Rural Community" (B.A. thesis, Indiana University, 1981). The Vincent essay was written for a W. E. B. Du Bois writing contest and is available through the Indiana University Department of History. He uses voluminous Roberts family papers submitted to the Library of Congress (copies in the Indiana State Library) to establish that having lived as free people since the late eighteenth century, and having migrated from North Carolina to Rush County (Beech Settlement) by choice, the Roberts extended family was well equipped to establish a successful community when virgin land became available in Hamilton County.

5. Norma Scott Johnson, Hazel Jefferson Adams, and Norma Williams Rice, eds., *The Pettiford Family Tree: A Genealogical History* (Los Angeles, Calif.: Published by the editors, 1983).

6. "Records Relating to the Enrollment of Eastern Cherokees by Guion Miller, 1908–1910," microfilm, 12 rolls (Washington, D.C.: National Archives and Records Service, 1969). The availability of this 12-roll series in the genealogy holdings of the Kokomo-Howard County Library should be of interest to those beginning their research in the index to the larger series of microfilms. Cataloged with the microfilm are two index lists, one alphabetical and one numerical by application number, that have been compiled by this writer by extracting the Indiana applicants from the master alphabetical microfilm index. (Copies of these indices are also cataloged with the Indiana Historical Society Library.) Because claims were assigned numbers in the order in which they were received, members of the same family filing individual applications do not necessarily appear in close numerical sequence. While these indices will be of assistance in identifying family groups, only the internal information in individual applications (see microfilm copy) and notations made by claims clerks on the covers of these applications suggest sibling and interfamily relationships among those of different surnames. Additionally, some applicants filed more than once, in their own right and also as guardians or executors for others.

Once an individual's application number has been determined, the appropriate roll from among the 348 related to the actual applications may be obtained. The major part of the material is available only from the National Archives, and restrictions regarding availability may arise.

7. Gaiselle Kerner, comp., *Preliminary Inventory of the Records of the United States Court of Claims,* National Archives and Records Service, vol. 58 (Washington, D.C.: National Archives and Records Service, 1953), 9. The clearest explanation of the several enrollments of Eastern Cherokees and conditions leading to the lawsuits is still Gaston Litton, "Enrollment Records of the Eastern Band of Cherokee Indians," *The North Carolina Historical Review* 17 (July 1940): 199–231.

8. See Russell Thornton, *The Cherokees, A Population History* (Lincoln and London: University of Nebraska Press, 1990), 46. Thornton says "(s)ince the Cherokees traced their descent along female lines, a child of a Cherokee mother and a non-Cherokee father was considered fully Cherokee, although children of Cherokee-black unions increasingly were not accepted unequivocally." Gary B. Nash, in *Red, White, and Black: The Peoples of Early America* (Englewood Cliffs, N.J.: Prentice-Hall, 1974), 296, says

(speaking of the mountainous areas of southern colonies and states), "in most cases they [the slaves] seemed to have disappeared into Indian society where they took Indian wives, produced children of mixed blood, and contributed to Afro-Indian acculturation in the same fashion as those slaves who lived with settlement Indians in coastal regions. So common was Afro-Indian contact in the Southern colonies that the term *mustee* was added to the Southern vocabulary in order to categorize the offspring of African and Indian parents."

9. The refusal of the Cherokees to return to slavery blacks living among them is complicated by the fact that blacks were often enslaved by the Cherokees themselves. Repatriation clauses in eighteenth- and nineteenth-century treaties with the Cherokees prior to the Removal Acts indicates the extent of the black presence among the Indians. Nash, in *Red, White, and Black* (p. 294), suggests that the inclusion of clauses insisting on the return of slaves suggests that the Indians were not responsive to other inducements such as bounties.

10. "Records Relating to the Enrollment of the Eastern Cherokees." This is the information appearing on the first several rolls of microfilm.

11. A casual review of county histories and other readily available publications yielded little information on J. R. Hadley. In the Grant County courthouse records of marriages, book 15, p. 271, there is an entry for the marriage of John R. Hadley to Alma A. Tibbetts, on 7 September 1904. It is apparent that he was an attorney in Grant County, but except for some briefly noted club affiliations by his wife, no other information was found.

12. The depositions of Jeremiah Shoecraft and Alvarian Shoecraft relate this incident, which is not further substantiated.

13. According to James T. Pettiford's testimony and that of his mother, he was the natural son of Clarinda Pettiford and Osborne Giles, and he was born in North Carolina and raised in the home of his grandfather, Edmund Pettiford. Recent compilers of Pettiford history and genealogy have suggested that James was a *son* of Edmund and Sarah Carter Pettiford; see Johnson, et al., *The Pettiford Family Tree.* Relying only on data from the 1860 Grant County census, which lists James as a dependent in Edmund's household, they could not determine how he was related. Anyone who might have had firsthand knowledge of his parentage is long dead, hence the importance of the documents under discussion here.

Index